THE NATURE OF GOODS AND THE GOODS OF NATURE

WHY ANTI-GLOBALISATION IS NOT THE ANSWER

Estefania Santacreu-Vasut
and Tom Gamble

SOCIETAS
essays in political
& cultural criticism

imprint-academic.com

Published in the UK by
Imprint Academic Ltd., PO Box 200, Exeter EX5 5YX, UK

Distributed in the USA by
Ingram Book Company,
One Ingram Blvd., La Vergne, TN 37086, USA

ISBN 9781845409784 paperback

A CIP catalogue record for this book is available from the
British Library and US Library of Congress

Dedicated to those who will come

In the last decades, millions of people have been lifted out of material poverty. And yet, the news seems to portray a different, far less encouraging picture of the world. At the political level, debate is moving from the right-left space into the open-closed space (or globalisation-nationalism divide) and political rhetoric is nurturing the idea that closing borders can be welfare-enhancing.

In this book, written as a story where an old professor and her former student meet in a bookshop to exchange memories and discuss current economic and political events, Estefania Santacreu-Vasut and Tom Gamble show that understanding the nature of goods sheds light on the challenges and opportunities that the goods of nature— human, social and environmental—offer to humanity, and how anti-globalisation is neither the solution nor the best way to address those.

Contents

Preface

Dear Reader, imagine that you enter a bookshop, a wonderful and living world of atmosphere, intimacy, and the heady smell of paper volumes old and new. You wander among the shelves, absently conscious that you're looking for something that will take you away on a journey. Your eyes flit across titles on brightly coloured book spines, you reach out to touch, you may inch one or two from their snug shelves and nudge them back with a fingertip until finally something really catches your attention. This book.

Something in the title of the book intrigues you. And, now that you have it in your hands, we invite you to remember the last time you sat in a café: what did you think about? Maybe it was how happy you were since you decided to quit smoking and take public transport—despite the poor quality of the air in the underground. Maybe, also, you were alert and fearful that a terrorist attack might happen at that very place and time, looking at those around you with a mixture of empathy and defiance. Or maybe, finally, you were just remembering the lovely spring afternoon when you walked in the countryside and plucked a few shoots from the wild flowers to plant in your own green space once home.

Imagine that, inserted in the pages at the back of this book, you find a ticket for a train ride to a small town in France. Someone must have forgotten they'd put it there.

The town has a very odd name: *Enfer*—which in English means *Hell*. Caught between unease and laughter, you have a look at the destination on your smartphone. It does indeed exist! And it looks a small and pretty town, with less than three thousand inhabitants, nestled cosily in the hills. Would you take that train?

You turn towards the bookseller and the cash desk, intent upon buying the book, when suddenly—who would have thought it—you hear a very familiar voice greet the bookseller. You turn, and there she is, stepping into the bookshop —your old Economics professor. Older, thinner, but unmistakably her and sporting a rather fine tan. Amazing! And then you remember something. What did she once teach you? Ah yes! Something about the nature of goods…

Chapter 1

What is a good?

I remember sitting in class and hearing this strange question: what is a good?

When my teacher asked that fatal question—the one I remembered years later when meeting her in the bookshop —I was in my late teens. It was naturally a silly time. We laughed at things I would never laugh at now. 'What is a good?' she had asked. And my mind, young and petulant, immediately thought: *'What is a Good if it isn't Bad?'* Answer: *'it's a Better.'* There, I told you—I would now never laugh at some of the stuff I once called humour. But it haunts me. The word *good*, that is. If only I had had the reflex to ask myself where this odd word came from. At first I assumed it was from the word *God*. But, years later, trawling the internet for an answer, I found that its roots were in Old English *gōd*, meaning virtuous, desirable, valid, suited—or again— having the right or desirable quality. Could it be that when we refer to our commercial goods this is what is meant? And why is it that in other languages, too, often the word used for something of good character and quality is also the same word we use for our goods, our products? *Biens* in French, *Gut* in German, *dobra* in Polish, *beni* in Italian, *bien* in Spanish. The world is a strange and magical setting for these tiny gems of discovery. It is also a stage on which the players of learning and curiosity hope to push us towards a truth. And that brings me back to my old teacher, that enchantingly serendipitous meeting many years on and the fact that it propelled me backwards in time when she spoke the wonderful jargonese of the economist. 'What is a good?' she had said. And the answer she had given, unplucking her glasses from her nose as she spoke, was — if I remember rightly — not at all bad.

'Goods: *they surround us!*' she had declared, glancing out of the lecture hall at the gathering grey clouds in the university park beyond. 'This evening you'll need an umbrella for the rain, and don't forget your jacket when leaving the classroom! Next term, you may get yourself a pair of sunglasses for the sunny days — if we're lucky with the weather, of course.' She smiled at us. 'How much do you pay for these goods? That's the question, isn't it? After all, both you — and I — are consumers who make choices…'

Back in 1995, the bible of microeconomics was published in Cambridge MA, USA.[1] Written by Professors Mas-Colell, Whinston and Green, the book introduced the theory of consumer choice in a market economy to the young and eager Economics PhD student. I vividly remember reading that we, as consumers, choose among various 'goods and services that are available for purchase in the market'. A good, therefore, is something we choose to pay for. It brings us well-being. Why would we choose it, otherwise? And it improves our life, instantly or in the long run. Think about the difference between an ice cream and a washing machine. Goods that provide us instant pleasure are called non-

---

1   Mas-Colell, A., Whinston, M.D. and Green, J.R. (1995) *Microeconomic Theory*, New York: Oxford University Press.

durable goods, while those that improve our well-being over time are durable goods.

'But Professor, there are many things we don't pay for that still do good to us, don't they?'

'Yes, there are things you don't pay for. Can you think of some examples? *What about time? And ideas?*' she had said. 'Yes, these are goods!' The class stared at her, as if she were asking a bizarre question, engaging them into the unknown perspective of a well-known field. They remained silent but concentrated. 'What about the rain that's falling right now? And what about the sunlight that you enjoyed during the gone summer days? And the wind that makes the leaves fall when October comes round… Are these goods?'

Our professor paused, letting the classroom breathe and think. It was autumn, and the day was coming to an end. She looked at us with a direct gaze. We were there, alive, tired after a long day at school, but captivated by the simplicity of the question she was asking. Those of us who were lucky enough to have mobile phones and computers switched them off. And then she sat behind her desk, smiled at us, and told us a story.

'A few years ago, my partner and I decided to have kids. It turned out I had become pregnant not with one but with two boys. When thinking about the education we would provide to our kids—Sasha and Max—sharing was an important value to us. Should we buy everything twice? We thought we shouldn't. After all, we wanted them to play together and learn how to share.

'Later, when the boys were a little older, one of our friends brought home a gift for them: a basketball. Sasha started playing with it, running through the corridors. They were too small to know the rules of basketball and they had never seen a basketball game. Max was running too, hoping to catch Sasha and get to touch the ball. We looked at them, amused, while having tea and pastries. Max rapidly became annoyed and upset, as he couldn't get the ball. They started competing for the same objective: getting possession of it, and playing with it. "Share the ball with your brother!" I told Sasha. But they would not: simply because they could not simultaneously hold it. That is, rivalry and conflict emerged as a result of our friend's gift. After they'd bickered and shouted several times, we decided to suggest that they watch a movie. And suddenly, both were sitting quietly, watching their favourite movie. Why? Because that was something they could do simultaneously. No conflict arose, and no rivalry either.'

The students looked at their professor, half-amused and half-wondering what the story had to do with economics. Well, as it turns out—a lot. Economists use the word *rivalry* to define the nature of goods. It does not denote conflict or competition, but rather it describes a good that, like the basketball, cannot be held or consumed simultaneously by several individuals at the same time! A good is *non-rival*, on the other hand, if the cost of providing it to another individual is zero. In other words, it costs nothing to allow another kid to watch the movie and, most importantly, adding another kid to the movie party doesn't change other kids' enjoyment. On the contrary!

'But, what about a basketball game?'

'Well, a basketball game is a set of rules, usually enforced by an impartial referee... in a game all players play with it, but only one can hold the ball at a time, and only for a limited amount of time...'

Whether a good is rival or not depends on its intrinsic nature and not on the institutional or political environment.

'Professor, does that mean that non-rival goods are free?'

'Not really. Even if watching a movie with your friends doesn't decrease your ability to watch it—it may even be more fun—your friends may decide not to invite you. In other words, non-rival goods may be accessible or not. The ability to access a good, or to exclude someone from accessing it, is the second key feature of a good. Economists call this the excludability of a good.

'Excludability relates to the rules that allow *certain* individuals to consume *certain* goods. And in a market economy, the price is the key mechanism that gives access to a good. When we think about the basketball, it's clear that unless we pay for the ball, we cannot claim either access to it or its ownership. Similarly, unless we pay or get invited to the NBA playoffs, we can't get into the stadium and enjoy the game. So, both the basketball and the NBA game are excludable. What about rivalry? Well, while only one player can hold the ball at any point in time, we can all watch the game simultaneously. That is, the basketball is a rival and excludable good. Economists call these types of goods *private*. The NBA game, on the other hand, is a non-rival and excludable good.'

'Are there other ways to control who has access to a certain good other than prices?'

'Yes. The state but also local communities often rely on other mechanisms. For example, they may regulate access to a certain good. Or, when a good is given for free, we usually stand in the queue to be able to get access to it. Waiting, we pay, but not with money: we pay with our time.'

'Can you give us an example of a good that is non-rival and that is sometimes excludable and sometimes not?'

'Yes. Let's think about it together. Today I came to work by car. I took a motorway. It turned out the motorway I took is free. There is no toll to access it. That same motorway, though, could be easily made excludable by adding tolls. This is a perfect example of a non-rival good that can be made excludable or not depending on policy choices.

Recently, the mayor of Paris made the streets next to the River Seine excludable. Cars can't use them anymore, not even if they pay! That is, using regulation, the mayor can restrict access to certain streets, either for cars or pedestrians.'

'But Professor, when there is a traffic jam, adding an extra car has a huge cost on others!'

'That's right. Certain goods are non-rival up to a certain point. That is, they may become congested. But we may be able to prevent congestion by making these goods excludable, like adding a toll to access the highway.'

'Are there any non-rival and non-excludable goods? Wouldn't that be paradise, professor?'

The professor smiled at her student's remark.

'If goods were non-rival and non-excludable, everyone would be able to consume them — non-excludable — at zero cost — non-rival. Would that be paradise?' she asked. 'Well,' she continued, before anyone could answer, 'it would be if everything we ever needed already existed and nothing had to be produced.

'Here, too, economists have a word for this type of goods: these are public goods. In fact, managing these types of goods may be quite difficult. We face a key challenge: no single individual has incentives to produce public goods. But what about a community? Indeed, the provision of certain public goods may require cooperation among individuals living in the same neighbourhood, while others may require the cooperation of the seven billion or more inhabitants of the planet Earth! That is, some public goods are local… and others are global.

'However, public goods and private goods are the two ends of the spectrum. In between, there are other types of goods. For example, private parks are excludable (only those granted access to the park are able to benefit from it), but they are non-rival. We economists call them club goods. Unless you're part of the club, you can't access them. Think about yourself, sitting in this lecture hall. You belong to the group of students who enrolled and because of that you have the right to access the lecture.'

'But professor, when we go out for a walk in the evening, we aren't consuming a good, right? If we are, I'll start seeing goods everywhere from now on!'

The professor sat down and, as was custom, said that it was a really interesting question. She decided to turn on the projector.

'I want to show you something', she said. And then she projected her calendar. In the notifications of her calendar it read: *Your evening seems free.* 'But is it really free?'

'No Ma'am!' I said. 'You could be teaching an extra hour of class.'

'Brilliant!' she answered, relieved to notice that her students were still awake at the end of the afternoon. 'Indeed, I could teach more and earn more. By choosing to have a free evening, I'm not really having it free! Words… beware of words! A free evening has a cost, even if hidden: the earnings I'm not making by not working an extra hour.'

'Isn't that what we call the opportunity cost?'

'Yes. By choosing not to spend an extra hour at work, I'm giving up my hourly rate. If that rate is very high, it means that I'm willing to pay a high price for my leisure time. What's the cost of your studies? Not only the student fees, but also the salary you aren't earning by not being in the labour market.'

A silence filled the lecture hall, everyone with their thinking caps on. And then, from the back, came a voice.

'Professor, I read that humanity is over-exploiting our oceans.'

'That's not really related to what we're discussing now', noted the professor. 'But yes—and that's the tragedy, even for economists and their jargon! It's called the tragedy of the commons. The commons are goods that are rival—if you eat a fish, your classmate can't eat it. But in some regions of the world, they *aren't* excludable. How to prevent overfishing, then? How to allocate those goods and avoid a tragedy?

'Economics is the science that studies how to allocate scarce resources to alternative ends. You may think that prices and markets are what economists study, but there are other mechanisms such as regulations, rules, norms and institutions that influence such allocation, even for goods that cost nothing to provide to the additional user.

'It's now time to end the class and enjoy your not-so-free evening! And remember, goods surround us! And every decision we make involves some kind of arbitrage or trade-off. How we, our neighbours and friends, our fellow citizens, and humanity at large manage to allocate them is a key issue for those of us who are here, and, most importantly, for those who will come.'

All those years ago, I remember sitting there at the end of the lecture and watching my professor pack her things, smiling at us. And I thought about what I had just learned. Some of the goods will bring us joy and happiness, privately. Others will bring well-being to our communities. Our communities? What defines them? Linguistic, religious, national or historical ties? What if the nature of goods defined us more than the other way around? And, what if understanding their nature would allow humanity to be truly united? If only… On the contrary, some goods, that we could potentially all enjoy, would surely be in the hands of a few. Not because of the nature of the good, but because of *our* nature and the rules and norms we impose upon ourselves and to others.

As the professor packed her own things and left the classroom, a student came to see her and asked: 'Professor, what is the world in which Sasha will grow up? What is the nature of the goods that we will give to our kids to play with in the future?'

'That', replied the professor, benevolently, 'is a good question. But one for another time, perhaps. The time it takes to turn over a new page.'

Key concepts

- Durable good: a durable good is a good that is consumed through several periods of time.
- Non-durable good: a non-durable good is a good that is consumed in one shot.
- Rivalry: characteristic of a good that describes whether the consumption of the good by one individual decreases the ability of another individual to consume it.
- Excludability: characteristic of a good that describes whether an individual access to a good can be prevented if the individual does not pay for it or through some other mechanism.
- Economics: science that studies the allocation of scarce resources to alternative uses.
- Public good: good that is non-rival and non-excludable.
- Private good: good that is rival and excludable.
- Club good: good that is non-rival but excludable.
- Opportunity cost: the benefit that is not received by taking a different action.

Chapter 2

How to allocate goods?

My teacher used to refer to the school cafeteria as a place where we were buying a very specific type of good to keep us awake: coffee…

'Wonderful!' I said, still under the shock of seeing her after all this time. 'Let's sit and chat. And I saw the bookshop has a coffee machine. Would you like to grab one?'

'What a good idea', beamed the old professor. 'This bookshop is lovely — my favourite in all the four corners of the world — and the bookseller is such a good friend. Let's sit here.'

The bookseller came over to our armchairs, acknowledged my presence with a hello and greeted my old professor with a hug.

'It's lovely to see you around here, Martha. It's been a while. And how's life in Chile? I'm envious, you know!' he joked.

The old professor laughed softly.

'It's lovely to be back, indeed. And yes, Chile's such an amazing experience.' She turned to me. 'I'm recently retired you know, and sheer chance just happened to put me onto the track of a lovely little house in Valparaiso, Chile. It's another life. And did you know — the famous poet Pablo Neruda once lived there!'

'Well, it's almost on the other side of the planet but I hope you'll still keep visiting!' smiled the book seller and then, as if remembering that he had two customers to take care of, looked at us.

'So, what would you two like to drink?'

'I'd like a green tea please', said the old professor.

'And you?'

'A regular coffee for me, thanks.'

Coffee. I love the word as much as I love the word tea. Both end with a lovely, warm *ee* sound, both have long histories, many qualities and sometimes, as some claim, even magical powers. In the tea-drinking countries I've visited, I witnessed the belief that the future can even be predicted by reading the signs left in the tea leaves in the bottom of your cup. Enchantingly, the same applied for the coffee-drinking cultures I've visited: gaze down at the dark brown deposit and the future is revealed. It's Monday morning, 10.30 am, and I'm doing just that—gazing down into my empty coffee cup and waiting for the bitter-sweet black magic to work and propel me to work. Unfortunately, I don't have the particular skills to read my future in the dregs of my cup, but I do know one thing about what is to come—it will be a very busy and exciting day ahead. Instead, letting my gaze wander about the bookshop and my thoughts percolate over my old professor, I'm reminded of a recent pre-holiday visit to Dublin, Ireland.

Dublin is a friendly city. One of the friendliest I've ever visited. And on my final morning there, caught up in the atmosphere of it all and with an hour to kill before taking the plane back home, I decided to sit in a coffee shop in the city centre and sip on a cup of the black stuff.

One of the particularities of this particular friendly shop was to ask its customers their first name. Standing in the

queue at the counter, I surely enough learnt that the two
people ordering in front of me were called Juliana and
Michael. And upon hearing their name, I looked at Juliana
and Michael in a different light. Michael's bright green
bobble hat, together with festive antlers, became in an
instant quite fun and charming. Indeed, it seemed to fit
Michael's face to a T. Likewise, my early morning moodiness
—always a feature until the brain manages to push
nascently, painfully into a fully-woken day—dissipated as
though an imaginary wand had been waved when Juliana
began chatting loudly to a friend on her mobile phone.
Students, I said inwardly and thinking of my own days of
study, *have a right to be loud and cheerful at such an unearthly
hour after all.* When my turn came, the vendor duly asked me
my name. Feeling rebellious, I immediately told him it was a
secret. After all, my name is my identity, I thought—and
mine to keep or offer as I wished! And for a moment both
the vendor, Michael and Juliana—waiting further down the
counter for their coffee to arrive—turned to each other in
shocked confusion. Seeing their consternation, I then smiled
and said:

'Can I make it up?'

'Well,' said the vendor, again taken aback but at least
over the initial shock, 'sure you can.' And before I could
come up with something the vendor added: 'Why not
Superwoman?'

This produced a burst of laughter from my fellow
customers and, not to be outdone and returning the vendor's
good-naturedness, I replied that it would suit me perfectly.
A few seconds later and the vendor's very loud voice
announced to the packed coffee shop:

'*Superwoman—your coffee's ready!*' The vendor even
served me with a radiant smile. And then, with a slight bow,
added: 'Madam, you are my hero.'

I smiled back and took the receipt. It was then that my smile instantly disappeared. *What? So expensive for such a tiny beverage!*, came a little voice in my head. *But then again*, came a second voice almost immediately, it *had been the most fun and friendliest coffee I'd ever been served* — it was worth it.

Sitting down and sipping my delicious syrupy coffee, breathing in the alchemy of its vapour, it came to me that I was, despite the difference in age between myself and most of the other customers, very much like them. Indeed, here was coffee being rationed to the same sort of people, all of them hovering not far from the nearby offices and university buildings. It was likely, I mused, that the same students now frequenting the coffee shop and writing up their assignments would one day be employed in the same nearby offices. This was not a fast and inexpensive coffee. But one that boasted its higher cost as the price to pay for the one of the friendliest, tastiest coffee experiences in the world. I wondered if such a brew could be sold on the supermarket shelves and quickly dismissed the idea — no, the friendliness would be absent. And it was hardly likely that my local supermarket shelf stocker would ever call me *Superwoman*. Perhaps, I thought, the tasty coffee sparking off a creative chain of thought, the government at home could actually get their hands on it and distribute the friendly cheerfulness through state-run coffee shops: happiness distributed for the wider good. And why not free?

Returning to my brew, I sipped and sighed, just as bitter-sweet a parody as the Peruvian liquid ebbing over my tongue. The coffee had come to me as much as I had come to it. And it had come far — through cultivators, mountain slopes, commodity markets, transport, roasting and taste-tests, pricing, and decisions of where and where not to distribute it and who and who not to offer it to. Gazing down into the tar-like sediment in the bottom of my empty cup, and just as my taxi drew up outside, I wondered how such a future for the lowly little bean had been made in the first place.

But as I entered the taxi, I realised I'd forgotten to withdraw any cash and asked the driver if I could pay with a credit card.

'Sure you can, Ma'am! We need to modernise you know!'

'Yes, but you know,' I replied, 'I like to be able to catch a taxi on the spot and actually pay with cash. I don't want these apps to know everything about me, where I go, or why…'

'Ah, if all customers were like you,' said the taxi driver, 'but they're afraid of waiting. They're afraid of scarcity you know!'

Scarcity… it made me think of the first definition of economics I came across as a student: '*Economics is the science that studies the allocation of scarce resources to alternative uses.*' How do we allocate those resources today? The question is relevant because of the scarcity of them. If there wasn't such a scarcity, there would be no need to think about how we allocate resources to alternative uses. Think about time, for instance. It is precisely because our time is limited that we struggle when making choices. And it is because of this that we wait in a queue to get our morning coffee—so annoying: except, perhaps, in the friendliest café I'd been to in Dublin!

Daydreaming and looking through the taxi window, I had remembered with nostalgia my school years. Waiting in line at the cafeteria was a chance to hang out with the professors and administrators of the school. Students, professors, administrators—we were all there waiting for our morning coffee or tea. And there was no fast track for professors, students or for administrators.

And there we were, back in the bookshop, sharing a moment and a coffee with my old professor.

'What a coincidence we met! Especially since I barely have the chance to come here anymore…'

'Yes, indeed. And to share a morning coffee! Do you remember that morning when I arrived late to class?'

'Yes, I certainly do', she said smiling at me.

And as I was sipping another coffee, it transported me to that very exact day ten years back.

Once, on a cold Monday morning, I arrived late to my microeconomics class. Markets, supply and demand, prices. As I entered, the professor looked at me. Boosted by my coffee, energised, I valiantly asked:

'Why don't markets help me get a coffee faster? Isn't my time a scarce resource as well? Isn't there a better way to allocate resources?'

My professor couldn't help but smile, and my classmates burst into laughter. It was a happy Monday morning. Maybe what encouraged me to be so daring was my teacher's style and pedagogy. She always tried to use everyday life metaphors, making us laugh and getting closer to abstract concepts and ideas. She allowed us to understand how markets allocate resources and grasp that while we were all so used to hearing that we live in a market economy, we had a lot to learn before we could apprehend what it is that markets exactly do, and why and when they are serving the common good.

Why didn't markets help me get a coffee faster? What did I learn? Well, I understood that waiting in line, in addition to paying for my coffee, was part of the so-called 'allocation mechanism'. But it could be otherwise—we could get our coffee according to how well we get along with the waiter, whether we remember his or her name and whether the waiter knows our name, or whether they belong to our family or friend's network.

But market exchanges require none of the latter. If I'm in a bad mood, I can barely say hello, nor smile nor look at the waiter, but I still get to buy my morning coffee if... I pay for it! But this also means the waiter can't refuse to serve me the coffee on the grounds, perhaps, of some dislike for who I am, what I represent, my age, gender, lifestyle, appearance. What a relief, after all!

Yet, while markets allow for anonymity in any exchange, it doesn't necessarily mean that market participants are anonymous to each other. In fact, certain types of market exchanges can only exist if the transaction repeats itself regularly. This allows the seller to build a good and solid reputation that allows the buyer to engage in the transaction with confidence and trust. Moreover, this is particularly important when the seller can potentially convince the buyer into believing he or she is selling a high quality good.

While I knew exactly what type of coffee I was getting at the cafeteria, and I trusted the vendor to do the job well, I always tried to learn their names. Indeed, even in anonymous market exchanges there is a bunch of cultural and social institutions that surround markets. Each one of us, with our titles and specific roles within the school, were more than mere coffee consumers. And I realised that what the famous coffee seller in Ireland was inciting from us was, in fact, our sense of identity. And what made me willing to pay more for that morning coffee was that for a few minutes I got the chance to change my identity and *become a hero*. My valuation of the good was at least as high as the cost I paid for it. Or in the jargon of my microeconomics professor, it was the fact that the marginal utility of the coffee was higher than its price, which is its marginal cost—that is, the cost of buying an extra coffee. Had it not been the case, I would rationally not have purchased it.

So the good is allocated to consumers that are willing to pay for it, until the consumer with the lowest valuation is indifferent, at the margin, between buying the good or not. While each individual consumer is actually taking the price of coffee for granted, in the aggregate the price reflects the marginal valuation of the consumer that is indifferent between buying it or not. On the seller side, coffee shops will be selling coffee up until the point where the marginal cost of serving an additional cup of coffee is equal to the price. And when the cost of producing an extra coffee exceeds the price of it, which in a competitive market the seller does not choose, then the seller stops producing.

In the aggregate, the price of coffee will also reflect the marginal cost of producing coffee by the coffee shop that is indifferent between producing an extra unit and not doing so. That is the beauty of markets! They aggregate decentralized information in a way that is efficient, allocates resources and produces them. So how come the Dublin coffee shop can sell coffee at a higher price than its competitors? Because they choose to differentiate from other coffee shops by providing a personalised service, calling you by your name, or giving you a new identity!

Economists have analysed the resulting allocation of resources as a function of its efficiency. That is, in answer to the question *could we have done better, collectively?*, one of the criteria they use is the concept of Pareto optimality. Pareto optimality tells us whether we can make everyone better off without hurting anyone. It turns out that markets are efficient at allocating goods such as a regular morning coffee. Why? Because the private benefit we get from drinking our coffee is all that counts in the decision to buy it or not.

Private goods, like coffee, that are rival and excludable, are therefore suited to be allocated in a market economy.

Is this the case for all types of goods? No. This isn't the case when some of the cost of producing the good, or some of its valuation, is paid for or experienced by a third party that is not part of the transaction. Because the buyer or the seller may not have any information about the third party cost or valuation, or simply because they may not care about it (or as my microeconomics teacher said, *they may not internalise it*), their decision reflects only their private valuation and not the societal one. In that case, market allocation may fail to allocate the good efficiently. For instance, the third party could compensate the buyer or the seller in exchange for them changing their behaviour and everyone may be better off. Economists call these side effects *externalities*, from the fact that there are some benefits or costs that are external to the transaction. What type of good is more likely to lead to these externalities? The answer: *non-rival goods*.

Remembering my departure from Dublin again, I was projected back to that taxi ride. As we were reaching the airport, a huge traffic jam had stopped us completely. The taxi driver started complaining about the fact that the road needed repairing, and in an effort to stay calm he decided to turn on the radio.

Music, a non-rival good!, I told myself.

But, as he listened to it, I suffered from it! True, I could have asked him to turn it down, or he could have been more considerate towards me and ask whether it bothered me. What about the road? Yes, it too is a non-rival good: several cars can use it without decreasing its availability to others, up until a point—congestion!

'Ah, if they made a toll-paying motorway to get to the airport', the driver had groaned.

Doing so would actually mean excluding drivers that are not willing to pay for driving on a higher quality and less congested road. That is, the nature of goods is something intrinsic, like the fact that if the driver turns on the radio, I have to listen to it even if I didn't make the choice to or get any value or compensation. How society decides to allocate goods, and whether society decides to do so at all, is defined by the rules society builds. These rules constitute our allocation mechanism, which has the ability to turn goods that were freely available (like a road) into payable goods (like a toll-paying motorway). That is, to make goods excludable. Making drivers pay for accessing the road is one way to achieve that. But there are others.

Indeed, not all transactions are allocated within markets. In fact, many of them aren't. Why? Because there are other allocation mechanisms that have been created by society. Sometimes these alternative ways of deciding who consumes what make sense, sometimes they do not, but they are the product of power relations or historical accidents. Think about firms. So many exchanges take place within firms and organisations. When professors get tired of queuing at the cafeteria they may go to the professors' lounge, where their department provides them with free coffee, and an area to relax before or after classes. It's thought that this increases informal exchanges between professors, potentially sparking research collaborations, or increasing the creation of a common identity and team building. In the context of a firm, sometimes, as the analogy of the professors' common room shows, but for other reasons, a company internalises transactions that the market could also do. Why is this the case?

Oliver Williamson, co-recipient of the Nobel Prize in Economics in 2009,[1] posed the question: when will a transaction take place in the market or within the boundaries of the firm? Depending on how specific the transaction is, the firm may decide to produce the input in-house and hire the seller of the good as an employee.

Some of these transactions, therefore, may fail to exist in the market, but take place within the company. Furthermore, some transactions that are allocated in the market do not lead to an optimal allocation. Why is that? Because the social valuation of the good is different, in some cases, from the private valuation of the good.

However, some exchanges take place neither in the market nor in the firm. That is, they take place outside of the private sector. They occur in the public sector at different levels: the state, regional government, international organisations, or community and family structures. Inheritance rules, for example, provide a legal framework for families to allocate resources across generations. They differ greatly across societies, and over time. For instance, before the French Revolution in some regions in France parents had to respect perfect equality among heirs while in other regions parents could freely give advantage to one of the heirs to the detriment of others. These differences have deep consequences regarding the motivation of heirs to study, work, marry, migrate or stay in the parents' house, or even how many children to have. Indeed, the intergenerational transfer of resources touches upon not only private goods,

---

[1]   Oliver E. Williamson—Facts, *Nobelprize.org*, Nobel Media AB 2014, 16 Jul 2018, [Online], http://www.nobelprize.org/nobel_prizes/economic-sciences/laureates/2009/williamson-facts.html.

like furniture or other types of wealth, but also upon public resources.

But there are other, subtler ways that society uses to allocate resources. By constraining or imposing a cost on individuals that deviate from what is expected, social norms are also a way to force individuals to make certain choices.

In short, what I remember from my microeconomics course is that *not one solution fits all*. Depending on the nature of the goods we want to allocate, one or another allocation mechanism is preferable. An ideological stance that is *pro-market* or *pro-state*, or that presents these alternatives as antagonistic, may be useful in the political debate but is certainly not accurate—because different allocation mechanisms present advantages in allocating different types of goods. It means that there is no best allocation mechanism in an absolute sense.

Key concepts

- Positive externality: benefit that affects a third party that has not taken part in the transaction.
- Negative externality: cost that affects a third party that has not taken part in the transaction.

Chapter 3

Goods that travel

My first voyage away from the town I grew up in led me to difference and led me to another country. Where would this train ticket take me if I decided to use it?

It reminded me of a classmate, Suzanne, and a challenge she had to overcome on her travels a few years back. The world was her meeting room. And never a month went by when she wasn't on some plane or another flying to a customer, a prospect, a conference. She knew, thanks to her travels, how to speak five languages, had a laptop, a smartphone, a tablet, credit and debit cards and wherever she went—Boston, Tokyo, Barcelona, Rio or Berlin—all she had to do was check in, do her thing, flourish her cards and pay. It was as simple as that.

And here she was, just landed in Morocco, on her way to discuss a partnership with one of the country's top suppliers of the finest oils and essences in the south of the country—when her taxi broke down on a stretch of long, deserted road between Casablanca and Marrakech. After the driver had made several failed attempts at starting the engine, she climbed out of the car and walked a short distance to sit under the welcome shade of a tree in a nearby orange grove, for the time it took for a replacement car to come along. Long minutes passed and Suzanne was just thinking how beautiful the landscape looked and how the early evening sun made the pink earth a soft shade of tangerine, when a man stepped up and startled her.

'Are you all right, Ma'am? Can I help? And my apologies if I frightened you.'

The businesswoman relaxed.

'No, thanks. My taxi's broken down. I'm just waiting for a new car to come along.'

'Ah – so you must be the lady they said was lost.'

'Lost?'

'Yes – the taxi driver. He finally got his car to start. And when he couldn't find you he left for the police station.'

Suzanne shook her head. A quick call and the driver would know that he should return. She searched in her pocket.

'Oh, no – I left it in the taxi! I'll just fetch my phone in the car.'

'And I'm afraid the taxi has left', the stranger reminded her. 'The driver tried one last time at turning the key – and it worked! A loose cable on the battery. Sometimes', confided the stranger, 'things are like that.'

'Damn – and my phone? My luggage?'

'Gone with him, it seems. But do not worry, Ma'am – everything will be safe in his hands. He is a good man.'

'This is terrible, a disaster', lamented the businesswoman. 'Nothing like this has ever happened to me in all the countries I've visited.'

'I'm very sorry', said the stranger, regretfully.

'Let me draw some money out and rent a car. Is there an ATM near here?' said the businesswoman, searching in her bag and flourishing her debit card.

'Well', said the man, scratching his head. He seemed a little embarrassed. 'If you go that way – west – there's one in thirty kilometres.' He nodded eastwards. 'And if you go that way, there's one in only twenty kilometres.'

'Only?' gaped Suzanne.

'Yes', smiled the man. 'We're very lucky here. There are some regions where—'

'I'm not interested in your geography lessons', she said irritably. 'What am I going to do without any money?'

'Well don't you have any cash with you?' frowned the stranger.

'This is absurd. People don't carry cash with them any-more—at least, not where *I* come from.'

'Well—I don't have any money either', said the man, pulling out the insides of his pockets to demonstrate. 'People here are lucky if they *do* have a little cash in their pocket! So I can't pay for a ride for you. But I do have something.'

'You do? You mean a car, a motorbike?'

'Oh no—neither!' smiled the man. 'But I do have empathy.'

The businesswoman couldn't believe her ears.

'Empathy, you say?'

'Yes', replied the man, unperturbed. 'My empathy tells me that I should help you. That once, many years ago, I travelled to see my uncle and his family in France and that something similar happened to me.'

'But how can you help with empathy?' continued Suzanne. 'You don't have a car, a mobile phone or even a bike.'

'Ah', intoned the stranger. 'But I have feet. And a good heart and a conversational tongue. So I will walk with you to the next village and there I will call upon the villagers' generosity to let you use a phone.'

They walked. The road was long. But it was not such an unpleasant ordeal as the businesswoman had initially thought. They chatted, commented on the beauty of the landscape and the wide empty horizon, talked about where they came from and what they did in life. Suzanne learned that the man had two daughters and a son—all of whom he was very proud of because they were good in their studies and later wanted to help others with the knowledge they would acquire.

But the problem, after five or so kilometres of walking, was water. It was very hot, very dry and the clothes she was wearing—fit for a business meeting—were of no use in the beautiful but arid environment they found themselves in.

'Do any cars ever come this way?' she asked at one point. 'I'm starting to feel very thirsty and very tired.'

For once the man did not smile, a sign that he was beginning to worry.

'Usually there are cars and trucks that pass once every thirty minutes or so. This time—strange—there aren't.'

'Is it dangerous?' asked the businesswoman.

'We have the landscape we see. We have the air we breathe', replied the man whose name she had since learnt was Allam. 'And we have the animals.'

'But how can animals help us? It's so hot. I'm beginning to have a most painful headache. I need water.'

'Well', said the man, stopping suddenly. 'The animals can tell us a lot. Look.'

The businesswoman followed his gaze. On the cracked tarmac she saw what looked like animal tracks.

'So what?'

'A fox and her little ones', smiled the man. 'Three of them. And haven't you noticed? The tracks are wet. They come from over there. And that means that there is water. Sometimes', added the man, ruefully, 'life is like that.'

Sure enough, some thirty metres off the road, in a sunken hollow, there was a rock pool with a bubbling spring. The businesswoman looked at the stranger and laughed, amazed at the wealth this simple pool of water offered. Carefully, they climbed the little face of rock to where the water sprang from its source — out of reach of the animals — and drank.

'This is something money can't buy', she said, smiling to herself — a personal joke.

'Drink well', replied the man. 'We have ten kilometres ahead of us yet.'

The road seemed endless, although, in reality, they were making good progress since their brief stop by the spring. The sun began to fall, at one point gaining in speed and making the horizon a festival of pink and violet. A soft, warm breeze picked up.

'It's very odd', said the man at one point. 'Today, there's an absolute absence of cars and trucks. Not even a cart! It is', he added, philosophically, 'as though our destinies were meant to meet and that there's a lesson in all this for both of us.'

No sooner had he uttered his words when Suzanne let out a shriek.

'Allam — look! *Catch it!*'

The man's eyes followed her outstretched hand and they both began clutching at the object fluttering in the air. Of all things — a banknote.

'Got it!' cried the businesswoman. 'Incredible!'

'A lesson', grinned the man. 'A message!'

Suzanne held the banknote between her fingers.

'One hundred Dirhams', she groaned. 'The equivalent of ten dollars. That won't get us far.'

'Were you expecting five hundred to come your way?' chided the man, softly. 'This banknote has most probably passed through a thousand different hands and twenty-seven different cities, towns and villages to reach you. Its value is inestimable. What's more, one hundred Dirhams will get us everything we need — and more! Come, the village is not so far now. Tea, cake and a taxi await us. Ma'am — what more could we want?'

Sitting at a table in the village square and sipping on the most delicious mint tea she had ever tasted in her life, Suzanne looked out over the village to the hills and the distant horizon now bathed in a darker shade of mauve. She smiled. Felt at ease with herself and her surroundings. Inside the café, Allam — no longer a stranger — was on the telephone, connecting to the taxi driver and the authorities and telling them that all was well. Value, she said to herself, thinking back on her ordeal, was all around her: the air, water, animals, luck, people, empathy, help and goodwill. Indeed, she added inwardly, as Allam came to join her for the taxi that would soon arrive, the debit card travelled with her, it allowed her to make value work. But not all the value that travels is captured in the card, she concluded, raising her glass of mint tea to toast her helpful friend. Some value can't be monetised at all.

As I reminded myself of my friend's story, a poem she had introduced to me back in our time at the university came to my mind: *The Road Not Taken*, by Robert Frost. Roads… In my introductory economics courses we never mentioned roads. But I soon understood that, without them, not only could goods not move very far, but *we* wouldn't either.

And although Suzanne's first reaction had been to dismiss Allam's explanation about the geographical conditions in the country, economists have long recognised that economic factors are both influenced by geography and shape it. The deserted road on which Suzanne found herself stuck was not only first a source of personal darkness, and later one of enlightenment for her, but also for economists!

Indeed, the first image I saw in my economic growth lecture stayed with me long after. Our professor showed us satellite pictures of different countries at night. Light density testifies of human activity. There is more light in places with high population density but also with high economic activity and income per capita.[1] Two country comparisons captivated my young mind almost instantly, as they required little jargon to be understood. Suzanne may have forgotten this during her trip, but I remember that she was equally amazed by it during our lecture.

'Isn't it amazing that political boundaries show so clearly from outer space?' she'd whispered to me, excitedly.

'Yes, it is. Could you imagine an alien watching us from afar?' I answered.

'You two,' the professor had said, sharply, 'stop all this chit chat…'

Our professor hadn't realised that we were talking about the images she was showing us and went back to her explanation.

'Satellite data, as I was saying before the chatterers interrupted, shows political divisions from a distance. While light density at night has increased spectacularly in South Korea from 1992 to 2008, North Korea has remained cloaked in darkness.'[2]

She then showed us the growth in light density in China from the year 2000 to the year 2009. Interestingly, the growth in light density was weaker in the coastal regions, and stronger in the interior regions.

'Isn't this what we call economic convergence?'

---

[1] Henderson, J.V., Storeygard, A. and Weil, D.N. (2011) A bright idea for measuring economic growth, *American Economic Review*, 101 (3), pp. 194–199.

[2] Henderson, J.V. & Storeygard, A. and Weil, D.N. (2012) Measuring economic growth from outer space, *American Economic Review*, 102 (2), pp. 994–1028.

'Yes, exactly. When poorer regions grow faster than richer ones, their levels of income are said to converge.'

'Is it always the case?'

'Not really. For instance, look at a similar map but for India.'

And indeed, in India, light density increased the greatest in the four biggest cities that concentrate most economic activity.

Economies, as individuals, choose (or sometimes fail to choose) certain roads that shape their economic geography and resulting reality beyond what can be anticipated. Indeed, India and China have followed very different infrastructure development strategies. While China has privileged the development of roads connecting middle-sized cities, India has focused on upgrading its highway network connecting the main centres of economic activity, a cheaper strategy overall but with consequences regarding the concentration of economic activity along the highway network called the 'Golden Quadrilateral'.[3]

Commerce is the most visible way in which goods travel in an economic sense. We buy goods, like our morning coffee, whose key ingredient was planted miles away and is transported to our neighbourhood coffee shop. Our coffee shop imports coffee, to our delight, and we indeed import many other things for our daily lives, prominently oil. Not only to fill our cars' petrol tanks... but because oil is everywhere in our lives!

Commodities like coffee and oil are traded on commodities markets and their prices fluctuate as a function

3   Alder, S. (2015) Chinese roads in India: The effect of transport infrastructure on economic development, *2015 Meeting Papers 1447*, Society for Economic Dynamics.

of demand and supply. Beyond raw materials and commodities, we exchange a variety of goods with neighbouring and far away countries, some of which we also produce and sell to other countries. Thanks to trade we get to discover goods that we did not know about and that become part of our habits to the point where we forget where they came from. Think about a tomato! Today it's the basis of the most universal Italian dish—pizza. And yet, it came from the Americas centuries ago.

But goods also travel in less obvious ways, and outside of markets. Multinational corporations and international organisations are an alternative way of moving goods around.[4] Indeed, during her revealing trip Suzanne was in Morocco trying to partner with one of the country's top suppliers of the finest oils and essences. If the partnership had worked out successfully, Suzanne might have had to move to the country to follow through the initial steps of the partnership. While moving goods around involves building roads and infrastructure, moving ownership around and building cross-national partnerships at the company level involves transferring managerial abilities around and managing diverse teams across time zones. Information and computer technologies have greatly facilitated this process but they haven't been able to replace physical presence. One of the reasons for this is that part of the process of transferring know-how and making economic progress travel depends on knowledge that is tacit and hard to codify.[5] Moving experts around may allow countries to adopt

---

[4] Antràs, P. and Yeaple, S.R. (2014) Multinational firms and the structure of international trade, *Handbook of International Economics*, 4, pp. 55–130.

[5] Santacreu-Vasut, E. and Teshima, K. (2016) Foreign employees as a channel for technology transfer: Evidence from MNC's subsidiaries in Mexico, *Journal of Development Economics*, 122, pp. 92–112.

foreign technologies more quickly because it may smoothen the understanding of the key challenges but also because it may signal the value of the technology.

When domestic consumers buy more foreign goods than what foreigners like to buy from domestic producers, a country has a trade deficit. How do countries finance this deficit at the aggregate level? They can either use their stock of foreign currency to buy these foreign goods, or they can borrow money from foreigners. Indeed, countries trade not only physical goods but also financial goods. These goods are what economists call 'securities' and their trade is the mirror image of trade in goods. When trading securities, countries do not exchange goods *per se*, but rather they exchange the promise to receive a certain stream of income in the future in exchange for some upfront payment today. How much are they willing to pay for such a promise? It depends on a variety of things.

How the flow of goods, securities and money are connected and whether these flows are evenly distributed or not is what we call 'national accounting' studies.

'We could have a full course on the challenges of building national accounting methodologies that allow us to compare economic activity over time and across space', I remember my professor saying. 'But instead I'm only going to mention global imbalances.[6]

'Global imbalances refer to a situation when the flows of goods and of securities or assets are not balanced across countries. For example, in the Eurozone global imbalances increased in the mid-2000s. Spain imported much more than

---

6   Bracke, T., Bussière, M., Fidora, M. and Straub, R. (2008) A framework for assessing global imbalances, *Occasional Paper Series 78*, European Central Bank.

it exported, and to achieve that the country had to borrow from foreign countries. To do so it had to export securities. In other words, it had to promise its trading partners that it would pay them back. And to honour their promises countries need to either start accumulating a trade surplus that allows them to pay back what they had borrowed, or they have to keep borrowing.'

'But, professor, isn't it unsustainable? I mean, if someone kept promising her partner to take her out for a movie but she keeps paying for dinner, wouldn't she become tired of such promises?'

'Ah! Indeed, countries need to honour their promises, and to build their reputation to make sure it does not cost them too much. Otherwise the couple may break up! And what would this mean in a macroeconomic context? It would mean that a country may lose its appeal and would no longer be able to borrow from other countries.'

'But the US has been borrowing for many decades, hasn't it?'

'Yes, because investors worldwide are willing to lend the country all this money, at a very low cost for the US. But crises do happen—in a couple, in a neighbourhood, in a village, in a country, and at the global scale. But their impact is temporary. Why? Because there is trust in how to respond to the crisis. For a couple, the expectation is for the "faulty" party to apologise, and to take action to remedy the damage. At the country level, there are also expectations about how crises are managed. For example, how central banks should react to a financial crisis, or economic downturn.'

'But professor, in Europe there was so much uncertainty about how the European Central Bank would react to the debt crisis!'

'Indeed. But it's because this was a young couple and the first crisis! As institutions create a history for themselves, then investors, consumers, managers and politicians are better able to anticipate their reaction to new crises. International organisations that gather policy-makers around the world are not only a place to exchange ideas about economic fundamentals like technology, growth prospects or energy related issues, but are also a place in which to build knowledge about each other, both in good and bad times, and form expectations regarding how different countries' national institutions, and international ones, would react in times of a crisis.'

In the lecture hall, Suzanne touched my shoulder and whispered to me:

'My mum always told me: what matters is not what happens, but how we react to it.'

I smiled at Suzanne as warmly as I could since I knew that her mum had passed away when she was young. Expectations, trust, promises... I never imagined that they had such a central role in economics and in explaining the relationship between countries and their exchanges.

But moving goods around involves not only individual consumers, technicians or private firms, and their expectations, but also states. Through their policies, states also influence these flows. More importantly, states may guarantee the well-functioning of those institutions that we rely upon to interact with each other with some predictability. But countries' policy-makers may try to influence the flow of goods and of capital in a beneficial short-term way that nevertheless hurts long-term economic conditions by damaging the functioning of institutions.

'Let me give you an example', said the professor. 'Let's think about it together... think about money. *Money!* Remember how we learned that when a country wants to buy more from the rest of the world than what it sells to the rest of the world, it needs to sell securities. In other words, it needs to sell promises that it will repay what it borrows today to finance its trade. But, sometimes, it has an alternative: use foreign currency that has been accumulated and that can be used to buy goods from abroad. Symmetrically, when a country exports more than it imports, it can use the surplus to lend more to the rest of the world, or it can simply accumulate foreign currency. Or it can do both! China for instance has both lent money to the US, by buying US government bonds (promises of the US government), and accumulated dollars. Indeed, for goods to travel, we need to exchange currency, as we do when we visit foreign countries as tourists, business travellers or as migrants. The exchange rate, the relative price of two currencies, will partly determine how costly it is to buy foreign goods. Policy-makers may let the price of their domestic currency be determined in the market for currencies. Or they may fix it. But fixing the price is not just announcing a certain price but committing to intervene in the market by buying or selling currency! If a country wants to live beyond its means it may be tempted to buy its domestic currency to make it more expensive. A more expensive domestic currency makes other currencies relatively cheaper, allowing the economy to afford foreign goods at a lower cost. But this tends to lead to a trade deficit. On the contrary, some policy-makers may want to grow through an export strategy. In that case they may try to make their goods relatively cheap for foreigners by making their currency cheaper.'

'Ah! Manipulation!'

'Indeed! Policy-makers may engage in manipulation, but in this case — *currency manipulation!*'

'Is there a limit to it?'

'Well, to buy your own currency you need to sell foreign currency! But if you run out of foreign currency reserves then you can't keep pretending your currency is stronger than it really is.'

'That is, you can't pretend you are stronger than you are, can you?'

'Yes — *exactly!*'

'But can you pretend to be weaker?'

'In principle, yes. But selling your own currency has other costs in the long run by creating inflation…'

As I remembered the professor's example, I couldn't help but think about Suzanne's experience in Morocco when a one-hundred Dirham banknote landed at her feet. She immediately calculated that the banknote amounted to not more than ten dollars and remarked that it wouldn't lead her to too much. But she'd forgotten that prices were different in Morocco! And as I remembered my friend's adventure, I realised that roads, in the end, are all about connection. Geographic, economic and mostly human connection. Getting us from point A to point B, the 'road taken' — whether known or new — makes, as Frost said so well, '*all the difference*'.

Key concepts

- Economic convergence: process of catching up between poorer economies relative to richer ones, where low income per capita countries grow faster than high income per capita countries.
- Global imbalances: refers to a situation where the flows of goods and the flows of capital are imbalanced, with some countries running large deficits with the rest of the world while other countries running large surpluses.

Chapter 4

Goods that do not travel
Visible and invisible frontiers

Who, even twenty years ago, would have thought that the world would turn out such a rich and exotic feast of language to savour?

Back in the bookshop, the old Economics teacher asked me how life had turned out. And as I explained, I noticed, enchanted, that she had adopted the same posture as she once had when listening to the answers of her students in class. Out would pop her question, always, it seemed, when we were least expecting it, and then she would wait, head slightly inclined to the right as though offering her ear, a trace of a smile on her lips as though reassuring us that whatever we said—both poppycock or sharp insight—was viable and matter for debate.

I told her of the place where I now worked. A place where every day I met and talked with people from over twenty different nationalities and cultures. In the corridors, meeting rooms and from inside offices one could hear a babble of languages, sometimes two or three, or even four— depending on the number of people in discussion—blend into one. A language that combined English, French, Spanish and German, sometimes Hindi, Italian, Arabic, Flemish and Mandarin too. Who, even twenty years ago, would have thought that the world would turn out to be such a rich and exotic feast to savour? And that question led my mind, while continuing to chat to the old professor, onto the parallel thought of someone who had once invented a brilliant idea —a *universal language*. The language, of course, was Esperanto. Everyone has heard of it. But hardly anyone speaks it. Why is that?

With 6,908 living languages in the world one might think that there was a need for such a thing as a universal language. Think of how practical it would be to be instantly able to communicate and be understood by anyone. And that's exactly what the inventor of it, Zamenhof, thought when living in the city of Bialystok, now north-eastern Poland, in the late nineteenth century. Back then, four languages were spoken on the street corners of Bialystok: Russian, Polish, German and Yiddish. And one day, probably listening to the babble of languages as he walked in this elegant eastern Babel, Zamenhof had a brilliant and very practical idea. A new, universal language—Esperanto. Not only would Esperanto save vast amounts of time in learning other languages, it would, he foresaw, be the perfect medium for creating harmony between different cultures and nations. Mankind-Womankind would be brothers and sisters, would be one—the modern-day equivalent of the internet, Twitter, Facebook, international student exchanges, the World Cup and other universal bringers together: the perfect international, cross-border (borderless even) product.

It took ten years for Zamenhof to finalise Esperanto. But its journey, the most difficult part, was only just beginning. It did not travel. It tried, but what Esperanto came up against were barriers—those that in his lifetime Zamenhof could see, and those that were hidden and invisible and far-reaching even beyond his life.

You see, some people just love their own language. After all, language is a mark of identity. And she who speaks identity, as it were, also speaks history and values. And laughter. And sadness. And love. It allows people of a certain similarity and togetherness to talk to each other and get closer. But not only is language something that brings us together, it also, as some argue, acts as a barrier. It protects. Going back in time, imagine if one tribe of people invented an incredible new tool or method. Their invention could be naturally protected from the ears and understanding of others.

Now Esperanto was, initially, acclaimed by many as a startling spark of genius that could facilitate and reassure people of different tongues. Unfortunately, for Esperanto, it soon met with second thoughts. There were those who saw it as a political plot to undermine their cause. There were others who thought that Esperanto would cause the monuments of their cherished language to fall. It was very nearly voted by a vast majority to be a language of the League of Nations after the terrible events of World War One. But the representative of one country vetoed it and that was enough, afraid that Esperanto would further undermine his language's position as a beautiful and influential tongue: French. There were also others who thought that countless hundreds of thousands of jobs would be lost (think of all those translators and interpreters, linguists, language teachers and publishing houses) by introducing such a universal language into their country. And there were simply those who thought that anything new and different was bad.

Esperanto still exists today, spoken by an estimated two million people in the world. It is not what could be called universal in terms of size and reach, but it sits aside all the other 6,907 languages on our planet. And thinking of Esperanto and its story, and the frontiers and barriers it came up against—all the time speaking to my old teacher who hummed and nodded encouragingly and politely to my words—it dawned on me that its story could perfectly be translated into that of a certain type of good: *goods that do not travel.*

'So how's your family?' asked my old professor. She knew my family quite well, since we'd had a graduation dinner party where several professors and friends joined my close relatives.

'I just saw them for the funeral of my great grandmother.'

'Ah, that's sad', replied the old professor, her mind perhaps dwelling for a second on her now own ripe age and time that was flowing so quickly. 'My sympathy. I remember her well from your graduation dinner party. Such a vivid and joyful character she was! I remember her telling me about her experience as a teacher for handicapped children. I was very inspired by her approach to teaching…'

And as she navigated her memories of my great grandmother, I navigated mine, half listening to her.

When I was a child, I used to visit her once a year. She was the second wife of my great grandfather, much younger than him, and she lived in a small village located on the French-Spanish Pyrenees frontier. A village where smuggling must have taken place at night during the Spanish Civil War. She worked as a teacher for mentally handicapped children before she moved to London with us.

'Do you like maths too?' she used to ask me when we played chess together.

Once, she explained to me how during the cold winters she had to climb the mountain with her skis to teach. I imagined her climbing to a little house where the children were waiting for her to arrive with her knowledge and, I thought to myself, also with her kindness. Sometimes she would bring some food with her but on heavy snow days, when she couldn't reach the isolated house, her knowledge could not travel to warm the spirits of the family that was expecting her.

Geographical factors, such as distance, ruggedness, but also climate conditions, may indeed act as a barrier that prevents goods from travelling. And as I imagined my great grandmother walking as the snow fell, unstoppable through the laws of gravity, I remember our old professor also telling us something about gravity. What was it?

'Good morning everybody!'

'Good morning professor!' we all shouted back.

'Today we'll study the determinants of trade. And my question is: *what determines trade?*'

To answer this question economists use the gravity equation.[1] This equation predicts the amount of trade between any pair of countries and is named after Newton's law of gravity, the physics equation that describes the force between objects due to gravity. Economic size but also trade costs explain how much trade a pair of countries engages in. Geographical distance has been used as a proxy for trade costs. Of course, the bigger the distance between two countries the bigger the transportation costs between them. Countries that are further away from each other may also suffer from higher communication costs because they may be culturally dissimilar. On the other hand, countries that share ties, such as sharing the same religion or political

---

[1] Tinbergen, J. (1962) An analysis of world trade flows, in Tinbergen, J. (ed.) *Shaping the World Economy*, New York: Twentieth Century Fund.

system, for example, tend to engage in more trade with each other, presumably because such ties decrease trade costs.

'But, professor, with communication technologies and declining travel costs, shouldn't distance matter less?'

'Indeed that's what we would expect. But the data suggest that distance still plays an important role, which is considered a puzzle.[2] Why does distance continue to matter today? One reason would be that countries' endowments — whether they have natural resources or not, for example — are stable. And since endowments influence trade, trade relations tend to persist. But endowments cannot fully explain trade patterns since a growing portion of trade happens between countries producing differentiated varieties of the same good. Economists have studied the role of other factors to explain trade flows between countries. For example, while countries sharing a border are geographically close, it may not be enough for them to trade. Think about North and South Korea. They do share a frontier but there is light only on one side of the border.

'Yes, sharing a border may not suffice because countries that have different political and legal institutions, but also different currencies or historical roots, may engage in less trade. Institutional and political barriers may undo the geographical benefits of a shared border. Any other ideas about what can explain the lack of trade between countries?'

'Maybe speaking a different language?' I said.

'Indeed, sharing or not sharing a common language has been studied by economists as one of the determinants of trade flows between countries...

---

2   Disdier, A.C. and Head, K. (2008) The puzzling persistence of the distance effect on bilateral trade, *The Review of Economics and Statistics*, 90 (1), pp. 37–41.

'More generally, language and cultural barriers may explain why geographical distance plays an important role, even today. These barriers may also explain why the pattern of trade relations is persistent over time. In fact, economists have shown that trade patterns persist across centuries.[3] How can we explain this? One potential reason comes from the persistence of consumer tastes. Our taste for different food or consumption goods may depend on our past consumption, explaining some inertia.'

'Why do tastes persist across centuries?' I asked.

'At the microeconomic level, the nature of goods may play a fundamental role. Indeed, some goods may be addictive. Think about coffee for example! I got into the habit of drinking coffee many years ago, when I was a student doing my PhD. I would spend long nights awake working on my thesis. Some of my friends say that I became addicted to coffee during those nights! As happened to me and to many other individuals, society may develop habits that originated decades and centuries ago and that become culturally ingrained.'

'So professor, what you're saying is that if sometime in the past we started trading with a nearby country, because, for example, it was cheaper to import goods from them due to lower transportation costs, this could explain why we keep trading with such a country?'

'Indeed, distant past trade may have a long lasting impact on our tastes and habits and could explain why we keep buying from those nearby countries even when distance is not nearly as important as in the past.

---

[3]   Campbell, D.L. (2010) History, culture, and trade: a dynamic gravity approach, *MPRA Paper 24014*, University Library of Munich, Germany.

'So, history matters because it influences the shaping of our habits, and because our habits are transmitted culturally from one generation to another. Researchers have compared the influence of history to the influence of velocity in the gravity equation, which in thermodynamics is called the dynamic gravity equation.'[4]

'But not all goods that we trade are addictive like coffee, are they?'

'You're right. Coffee, cigarettes, oil are addictive goods, but not all the goods we trade are. Yet, our habits develop not only out of addiction but also out of experience.'

'Are we just lazy or afraid of change, or is there an economic rationale for this development of habit?'

'Very good question. From an economic point of view, it may be more efficient to develop habits that allow us to save time and effort in assessing the quality of new goods. It may also save us time searching for goods we like. Furthermore, we, our parents, grandparents and our ancestors more generally may have invested time and resources in learning how to use certain goods in the past, and it may be efficient to keep consuming those goods to use that knowledge. So our habits may reflect our own experience but also our collective cultural capital.'

'But professor, in our microeconomics classes we take consumer tastes for granted.'

'Indeed, from today's viewpoint we take our habits and tastes for granted and that is not a bad assumption in the short run, since habits cannot be easily changed in a day or two. And if you ever tried to change your habits then you must know how hard it is even though it's not impossible!

---

4   Campbell, D.L. (2010) History, culture, and trade: A dynamic gravity approach, *MPRA Paper 24014*, University Library of Munich, Germany.

Our tastes are predetermined today, but reflect past trade relations to the extent that those relations have shaped the formation of our ancestors' habits and our own habits.'

'So when we isolate ourselves from others we increase the likelihood that we'll be isolated in the future and that we'll stick to a predefined sense of identity because our habits won't evolve.'

'Exactly!' beamed the old professor. 'Cultural conservatives are one of the groups that lose the most from trade—because ancient trade influences our tastes and culture which influence our decisions today!'

'Is this why we're seeing a come-back of identity-based politics nowadays?'

'Maybe, but let's keep that on the back-burner for the moment and we'll come back to discuss that later on.'

I remember that during the break one of my classmates voiced the concern to our professor that we were entirely missing one important dimension on trade: the role of firms. How right she'd been. Indeed, trade also flows within multinational firms. Multinationals invest a large amount of their resources in acquiring knowledge about local markets, foreign consumer tastes, customs, languages and local regulations. These investments allow multinationals to be more productive today but also in the future, developing their brands internationally and their reputation, which moreover allows them to sell at higher prices than their competitors or to be perceived as providing higher quality goods. Indeed, one of the benefits of trade agreements is that consumers have access to a wider variety of products and higher quality goods.[5]

5   Berlingieri, G., Breinlich, H. & Dhingra, S. (2018) The impact of trade agreements on consumer welfare—evidence from the EU common

Trade today, therefore, is influenced by historical trading patterns, through the influence of those patterns on the habits and culture of individuals and on the experience or learning by doing acquired by multinational firms.

'How can those habits change then?'

'Well, wars or trade shocks that disrupt trade today do change future habits and have long-lasting effects. By changing trade patterns, wars have an impact on consumption patterns and habit formation. A war, and even a "trade war", may be detrimental not only in the short run, by reducing trade, but also in the long run by changing the habits of consumers. Subsequent trade may reflect those changes, even when the war is over.'

'Are there other more positive ways to change our habits?'

'Migration flows between two countries may expose us to new goods and allow us to develop new habits and increase trade flows. Do you remember that we talked about tomatoes? Well, tomatoes are part of a broader history of exchange called "The Columbian Exchange". Thanks to Christopher Columbus in 1492, tomatoes are one of the key fruits of Italian cuisine.'

'But the Columbian Exchange led not only to exchanges of food crops and to the exchange of ideas but also to the exchange of disease!'

'Absolutely, you're right. There were positive and negative aspects of the Columbian Exchange. For instance, while population losses in the Americas are hard to measure with precision we know that they are close to 90%. These

external trade policy, *Journal of the European Economic Association*, jvx053, https://doi.org/10.1093/jeea/jvx053.

losses explain, in part, the massive migration inflows into the Americas. The other reason is that the Americas were an ideal place to grow coffee and sugar in the fifteenth century. Prices of coffee and sugar fell due to the increase in supply and profits increased.[6]

'Researchers argue that these changes contributed to the occurrence of the Industrial Revolution in Europe[7] and had an influence on world populations. For instance, on the good side crops like potatoes had a positive health influence while tobacco had a negative health influence worldwide. Quantifying the costs and benefits is a daunting challenge, especially because not all of the consequences of these exchanges were direct. Many consequences were indirect and long-lasting, impacting how societies organise. For example, forced migration out of Africa through slavery, with more than twelve million slaves, influenced Africa in a long-lasting multi-dimensional way. It divided the population and had a negative influence on its political, economic, social institutions.[8]

'But migration inflows to the Americas were not only forced, as with slavery, but voluntary as well. Especially during the nineteenth and twentieth centuries, there was a surge of migration inflows in both North and South America of populations coming from Europe.'

'So professor, many Europeans themselves were migrants not so long ago…'

'Indeed!'

---

6   Nunn, N. & Qian, N. (2010) The Columbian Exchange: A history of disease, food, and ideas, *Journal of Economic Perspectives*, 24 (2), pp. 163–188.

7   Crosby, A.W. (1989) Reassessing 1492, *American Quarterly*, 41 (4), pp. 661–669.

8   Nunn, N. & Wantchekon, L. (2011) The slave trade and the origins of mistrust in Africa, *American Economic Review*, 101, pp. 3221–3252.

'So isn't it strange that there are so many Europeans today backing the rise of extreme parties that are anti-migration? Why do they argue that immigrants fail to adapt to the new environment, both culturally and economically, while their own ancestors managed to adapt to new environments in the past?'

The professor raised her eyebrows and sighed. 'This is an issue that researchers have explored deeply, but it's time to go now. We'll continue next week!'

'Would you like another cup of coffee?' asked the bookseller, waking me from my memories.

'Sure. Thanks!'

'So how is the shop doing? Are you still organising events?' my old professor asked him as I sipped my third coffee.

'Yes we are', replied the bookseller. 'The latest event was related to the experience of female immigrants and the challenges they face in their host countries.'

'That's an interesting issue!' the old professor exclaimed. 'Populations of female immigrants have been increasingly studied in economics research, especially in relation to their participation in the female labour force.'

'It's an important economic decision for them: whether to work in the formal labour market or not', said the bookseller in earnest.

'Importantly, it's not only driven by economic considerations but also by cultural norms related to gender identity — whether women should stay in the household or participate actively with markets and institutions. We had a team of researchers present their latest work on the issue and they shared ideas that were quite provocative but the audience was fascinated! They presented their historical research concerning the US.[9]

'The US is an interesting context to explore this question because it experienced two distinct waves of migration. The first wave came from Europe during the Age of Mass Migration and took place in the late nineteenth and early twentieth century. The second wave, more recent, originated from Asia and Latin America.

'The researchers explained that part of the changes in the origin of migrants throughout the twentieth century is the result of changing policies—with migration quotas by country of origin—and of changes in the cost of moving due to technological innovations.

'Throughout the twentieth century, females entered the US labour market in massive numbers, as well as in many other countries around the world. Did female migrants in the US experience the same phenomenon? Did their behaviour mimic that of US-born women? Answering this question is difficult because migrants often carry a stigma from being migrants and because the modes of entry into a new country are themselves gendered.'

'But one could compare migrant women with other migrant women coming from different backgrounds, couldn't we?' I asked.

'Yes!' nodded the old professor, vigorously. 'One key issue is to be able to distinguish whether migrant women work more or less because of their economic background or cultural origin. But comparing female migrants as a function of their country of origin doesn't allow us to distinguish between those factors. To achieve that economists have

---

[9]   Fernández, R. (2007) Women, work, and culture, *Journal of the European Economic Association*, 5 (2–3), 1 May 2007, pp. 305–332.

recently focused on one cultural factor that can help in distinguishing between the two: language.'[10]

And as the bookseller and my professor continued their exchange, I was transported back to one of the lectures I remember the most. It was about the relationship between language and economics.

'Language? What does language have to do with economics?' I'd asked.

To answer my question, the professor began to discuss how language is, in fact, *a technology*. This was just one of the fascinating insights on the link between language and economic outcomes.[11] Indeed, language is one of the earliest technologies that humans used to convey information beyond the 'here and now'. To convey information a language's grammar establishes sets of rules that force speakers to convey certain types of information, even if they do not wish to do so. For example, in French grammar, because words are divided into masculine and feminine, we convey whether the friend with whom we're going to watch a movie is a girl or a boy, while we may well prefer *not* to reveal this information.

'But why do certain languages force speakers to do that and others don't?'

'Well, our ancestors may have collectively shaped which features to codify in the grammar, and which not to, because these features were more important or salient in organising

---

10   Gay, V., Hicks, D. & Santacreu-Vasut, E. (2016) Language and gender roles among immigrants to the US: A historical perspective, in Paoloni, P. (ed.) *Studi di Genere: Il Mondo Femminile in un Percorso Interdisciplinare*, Rome: Edicusano.

11   Mavisakalyan, A. & Weber, C. (2017) Linguistic structures and economic outcomes, *The Journal of Economic Surveys Early View*.

their social relations.[12] Indeed, existing research has traced gender-grammatical distinctions, like whether a language distinguishes gender in its grammar (she/he) or not, to historical agricultural practices that shaped the division of labour between men and women.'[13]

'But those practices may no longer exist today. Why would language carry their testimony?'

'Even if those historical practices may no longer be relevant, language may still categorise those distinctions because language is a specific type of technology: a *network technology*. The key characteristic of a network technology is that its value depends on the number of users and that it is hard to change individually.'

'And is there any evidence that these distinctions influence economic outcomes today?'

'Well, there is evidence that these distinctions correlate with gender inequality. Why that is the case is a matter of ongoing study and debate. One reason though may be that a language's grammar helps us categorise our social environment and define our own identities, as cognitive psychology suggests.'[14]

'But why don't we get rid of grammatical rules that are no longer relevant?'

---

12 Galor, O., Oded, S. & Özak, A. (2018) *Geographical Origins of Language Structures*, 5 January 2018, [Online], https://ssrn.com/abstract=3097220 or http://dx.doi.org/10.2139/ssrn.3097220.

13 Alesina, A., Giuliano, P. & Nunn, N. (2013) On the origins of gender roles: Women and the plough, *Quarterly Journal of Economics*, 128 (2), pp. 469–530.

14 Boroditsky, L., Schmidt, L. & Phillips, W. (2003) Sex, syntax, and semantics, in Gentner, D. & Goldin-Meadow, S. (eds.) *Language in Mind: Advances in the Study of Language and Cognition*, Cambridge, MA: MIT Press.

'Ah!' exclaimed the professor, 'there you're touching on a very controversial and political issue! An important fact to consider is that, while languages change, they do so slowly. And it turns out that, according to linguists, gender is one of the most stable features of language.[15]

'Economists have studied how female migrants coming from the same country but speaking different languages behave in the US labour market. In the context of waves of migration to the US, existing work has shown that immigrant women who speak languages that have more gender-based distinctions in grammar do have lower labour force participation — in the past as well as today.[16] Perhaps surprisingly, this finding is not the result of specific migrant populations and specific periods but holds throughout the twentieth century despite the changes in economic, technological and migratory patterns experienced.[17] The association is not a historical accident and will certainly be deeply explored in the years to come. But there is controversy regarding the claim that language has a causal impact. Indeed, it is difficult to identify the causal impact of languages' grammars because societies that are culturally close to each other share languages that belong to the same linguistic families or that have influenced each other through language contact in the past. And the mechanism at play is still a matter of extensive inquiry including methodologies

---

[15]   Wichmann, S. & Holman, E.W. (2009) *Assessing Temporal Stability for Linguistic Typological Features*, München: LINCOM Europa.

[16]   Gay, V., Hicks, D.L., Santacreu-Vasut, E. & Shoham, A. (2017) Decomposing culture: An analysis of gender, language, and labor supply in the household, *Review of Economics of the Household*, pp. 1–29.

[17]   Gay, V., Hicks, D. & Santacreu-Vasut, E. (2016) Language and gender roles among immigrants to the US: A historical perspective, in Paoloni, P. (ed.) *Studi di Genere: Il Mondo Femminile in un Percorso Interdisciplinare*, Rome: Edicusano.

like experiments and combining other multiple approaches from various fields such as economics and cognitive psychology, among others. But increasingly, quantitative studies are confirming the finding that language matters.

'So languages help us communicate and get closer to others, but they also shape individual, social and cultural norms that may draw us apart. They may do so because we use language to categorise ourselves, others and unconsciously impose barriers on our identity and behaviour even when the environment changes.

'Goods may not travel, therefore, because of visible and invisible barriers. Surpassing those barriers has been a recurrent feature of our human history, with some very negative consequences, like the decimation of native American populations, but also some very positive ones, such as the opportunity for women to have access to economic life, and, as a consequence, to political life. Contact through trade has allowed mentalities and cultures to evolve and change because, decades and centuries back, trade shaped who we are in a way we tend to forget. Through our ability to exchange with others, cooperating or entering into conflict with others, we mould our identities, and our ability to change.'

Key concepts:

- Gravity equation: in economics, the gravity equation refers to the empirical pattern that describes trade between a pair of countries as a function of economic size and distance.

Chapter 5

Ideas and innovation

I looked up at the ceiling to the cave and saw the most beautiful paintings… and remembered how my ancestors invented things, travelled and bartered… thirty thousand years ago…

'There are moments in life when you stand in awe in front of a monument, statue or fine work of art and you understand that humankind has such an agile and inventive imagination', said my old professor, with the same slight smile she had worn on her face all those years ago. 'A creativity that sparks the body, hands, feet or fingers to craft something unique. There are other moments when, sitting on a crowded bus or commuter train, your eyes are caught by a face that's vaguely familiar and you slowly realise that, although not a friend or acquaintance, the person your gaze has fallen upon bears a resemblance that might indicate that he or she once belonged to the same family lineage, the same place, the same origins as the good friend you know. It is the kind of awareness that brings on a sudden flow of happiness and that leaves us with a lingering trace of melancholy and sadness. And it is in these moments that we realise that time has passed. And that certain things are destined to be lost.

'I once knew an Englishman whose life was changed by an encounter with such a moment. I remember meeting up with him, several years ago, after a time of going our separate ways. We were both in Paris attending a conference and, during the lunch break, we stole off to a café to have lunch together and catch up on lost time. Quite out of the blue we got onto the subject of that moment. The outcome of which, he confessed, his gaze peering into some unknown horizon, had always been embedded in his childhood dreams. His name was Peter. And Peter was now making his living as an archaeologist.

'Peter had come to France when he was twenty to study the language and at times, when he wasn't finishing off his assignments, often put his bike on a train and headed out of the city to the countryside. On one such occasion, he set out intent upon exploring the Dordogne region, which his French friends often referred to as one of the most beautiful regions in the country.

'They weren't wrong. Rolling hills, lush meadows and cosy, stone-built houses. It reminded him of certain parts of his own country — the Cotswolds or Kent, for example — but with sunshine! Stopping off in a small village, he noticed a large number of coaches parked in a special area marked by a billboard with a large red arrow and letters. They read: CAVE THIS WAY. With time on his hands, he decided to join the queue of sightseers. He paid his entrance ticket and after some minutes a guide ushered him onto the tail-end of a group of very old and very elegantly dressed Japanese seniors. As the line advanced in a shuffle and disappeared underground, a series of ghostly gasps of awe floated out of the hole in the earth and reached his ears. *Old folks are so easily impressed!*, a thought went through his mind: *as if they'd become children again!* And then Peter himself turned the final corner of the entrance tunnel and stepped into the wide, beautifully lit cavern. He drew breath, held it as his heart missed a beat. And then it escaped him in a gasp of awe, just as it had the thirty or so distinguished Japanese pensioners before him.

'He looked up at the ceiling to the cave and saw the most beautiful paintings: bison, horses, wild boar. And strangely, as though sucked back through time to connect with the past, he seemed to remember how his ancestors invented things, travelled and bartered… thirty thousand years ago. He would have loved to sit there for hours and stare in wonderment. But, their thirty minutes up, another line of tourists came shuffling into the cavern and a guide, holding a flashlight, waved for them to leave.

'Peter stepped back out into the daylight and for several seconds he closed his eyes. When he opened them, having got used to the glare, he caught an old Japanese man dressed in a navy blue blazer looking at him. The old gentleman had been in front of Peter in the cavern and had most probably heard his gasp as he'd looked up. Stepping stiffly up and back onto the tourist coach, the old gentleman stopped for a fleeting second and sent the young Englishman a complicit wink.

'Peter watched the coach start up and drive away and his gaze came to rest on a small hill beyond—a rounded patchwork of freshly ploughed fields and fallow grassland—slightly to the right above the cave entrance and a kilometre or so away. A good place for a spot of lunch, thought Peter, and immediately set off on his bike.

'With the images of the cave paintings still vivid in his mind, he reached the top of the hill in seemingly no time. He dismounted, propped his bike against a tree and sat down with his packed lunch and bottle of water by the side of a field. He chomped. He looked out into the pretty country-side. He drank. He chomped again. And sighed. A sigh that spoke of perfect peace and satisfaction. And then his ankle began to itch—probably an insect. He looked down. But instead of focusing on the tiny, reckless ant on his skin, his eyes moved instantly to something beige and almost yellowish in the ploughed earth beyond. Some sort of small, cone-shaped stone. His curiosity raised, he leant closer, peered, wrapped his sandwich up again, placed it aside, and bent forwards to pick the object up. *Curious*, was the first word that came to his mind. *Odd*, the second, as he looked at the object from all angles. Four centimetres long, with three facets on one side, wide at the base and pointed at the end, its edges tapered and finely serrated. Something, his mind concluded, weighing up the evidence and computing an answer, that would certainly have made a very good arrow tip indeed.'

Back in the bookshop, the professor paused in her story to take a book from the shelf. All the while absently reading the blurb on the back cover, she added:

'It was an object Peter recognised as man-made, intricate, perfect, industrial… A beautifully crafted object. And how it disappeared with the coming of new discoveries and innovations!' The old professor's voice was so earnest, so filled with enthusiasm that I had to laugh. 'So that was his moment', continued the old professor, not the least taken aback by my laughter. 'It led him to the local museum and the curator who congratulated him and who explained what he had actually stumbled upon.'

'An arrow tip', I said, teasingly, sure that my professor was chomping at the bit to say more.

'But not just any old arrow tip! No,' she went on, pausing slightly to open the book in her hands, 'a perfect example of industrialised manufacturing—what Peter later explained to me was called the *Levallois technique*.'

'The Levallois technique…', I said, dubiously, trying to hide my ignorance.

'You see,' added the professor, deciding to close the book and place it back on the shelf, 'as long ago as 500,000 years before our time, our ancestors actually perfected a working technique with flint that followed a series of processes. Which means, and which Peter made me discover to my amazement, that they had to think ahead several steps, taking a chunk of flint—what's called a core—and starting from a concept in their minds of what the flint tool would end up as. Apparently, the top of the core was lopped off—like this!' said the professor, suddenly making a swishing movement with her hand. 'And then, facet by facet, around and around the core, they broke away the flint. Like this', she continued, more subdued, carefully slicing off a series of imaginary shards. 'From these intricate patterns they produced perfectly symmetrical, three-faceted flakes.'

'Impressive', I said—and it was.

'Yes, but Peter went on to say that it created a lot of wasted flint. And time to train oneself and others to use the technique too. And that's why, in places where flint was rare or people just didn't have the time—or even because they were just plain lazy—this innovative method of manufacturing died out. Replaced by other innovations in technique—quicker, less intricate, more practical, and', added the professor, her voice dropping almost to a note of sadness, 'much uglier in many cases.'

'Huh—modernity!' I said, jokingly. 'Consumerism!'

The professor looked up, acknowledged my lightheartedness with a grin, and added: 'It's been a subject of debate and a headache of a question for thousands of years for us economists. Do you throw in more resources to produce more? Train people to work faster? Or let innovation and technology kill off the old ways? A lot of people in today's world would prefer to avoid the latter. It's scary. New. And most probably our ancestors thought the same.'

The professor paused, perhaps aware that her voice had sounded once again like that of the lecturer she once was for me. She raised her eyebrows. 'Personally, I'm all for ideas and innovation—with perhaps an exception when I think back to the moment Peter discovered that old arrowhead.'

At this point, my old professor turned slightly and, although her gaze returned to the bookshelves, her mind had obviously strayed back to her conversation with Peter and their memories. It took me back too. Back to my student days, my friends on the same programme, and the time I made dinner for them after returning from a week's holiday break—coincidentally in the Dordogne with its hundreds of amazing archaeological sites open to visitors.

The evening of the meal I'd gone to my cellar to look for a bottle of Cabernet-Sauvignon bought during my trip to the Dordogne region. I remembered that in France a wine cellar is also called a *cave*—a *cave à vin*. As I served my friends a glass, and as I was sharing my impressions about my holiday with them, a friend called Jonathan prompted:

'You know, I wonder if the men and women who drew those beautiful bison in the caves had a better life than ours.'[1]

'Well, they certainly didn't have better wine than ours!' I proudly answered.

'They couldn't, that's for sure, because the agricultural revolution was still to come.'

'Ah. Revolutions! Do you remember our economic growth lectures?'

---

1   Diamond, J. (1987) Agriculture: The worst mistake in the history of the human race, *Discover*, [Online], http://tinyurl.com/dl20161210a.

'Yes, and that example about the chocolate cake? Did your grandfather eventually reveal his famous secret recipe?'

I'd forgotten about that anecdote and as I went back to the kitchen to get some snacks the memory of the old professor came back.

'Good morning everybody! And welcome to the economic growth course. Now, the study of economic growth deals with some of the most fascinating questions in the social sciences. What are the determinants of economic growth? Why do some countries grow faster than others? Why do some countries lag behind while others catch up? But it's also an inquiry into human history, and a humbling one, as you will understand by the end of this course.

'To study economic growth, for a country or for a region or group of countries, we need to understand the process that leads to an increase in the number of goods and services that is produced over time. And the production of goods and services requires the use of what economists call "inputs". What we, collectively, put in creates output, or what is put out through this process. Who can think of a simple example of such a process?'

That morning I had come to class with a chocolate cake I'd cooked to celebrate a friend's birthday. As its smell emanated from my backpack, and having had no breakfast that morning, I took out the cake and, putting it on top of my notes, said:

'Do you think this could be an example?'

Most students laughed, but the professor simply smiled and said:

'Let's think about it all together. What type of inputs did you use to bake the cake yesterday evening? Baking a cake involves a variety of inputs', continued the professor. 'The first input you need is an oven! The oven is what economists call physical capital. The second input you needed was yourself! Your effort in baking the cake, and the time you spent cooking (instead of studying macroeconomics) is what economists call labour. In fact, if you have experience or learned how to cook from your elders, we'd call your input not labour but *human capital*. Now, the difference between labour and human capital is that the former is a flow, while the latter is a stock. Our human capital is the result of past investments to acquire new skills and it changes slowly over time. How much human capital we have may increase because we train ourselves, either on the job, or through formal educational programmes, or learning from others. On the contrary, it may decrease—or what economists call *depreciate*—because we forget what we learned in the past when we do not use our knowledge or skills. For example, next year you might forget part of this course!'

We all smiled, knowing that what our professor was describing was indeed true.

'So are we ready to bake the cake? Or is something missing?'

'Well, we need the ingredients, professor!'

'Yes, we need chocolate, flour, water, salt, sugar. These are what we call *intermediate inputs*. And these are the goods produced in other branches or sectors. We call them intermediate when they're not destined for final consumption but instead when they are used in the production process of another good. Is that all?'

'We need a recipe!' I said.

'Exactly. The recipe gives you precise instructions about how to mix the different inputs to produce your cake.'

'Where did you get the recipe from?' asked Rob, my fellow student.

'From a cookery book', I replied. 'I called my grandfather to ask him to share his secret recipe, but he mumbled to me: *just come over Friday evening and I will bake you one.*'

Indeed, my grandfather had himself inherited this recipe from a relative who owned a bakery famous for its chocolate cake. He may tell the recipe to me one day, as they had with him in the past, but he did not on that occasion.

'So some of these inputs that are available to us today are the result of current choices, like how many intermediate inputs we decide to buy, but also of past choices, like how many ovens did we buy or how much experience in baking cakes we accumulated in the past.'

'So does history matter?' asked my friend.

'Yes! And the inquiry about the sources of economic growth is an inquiry about the potential for our current choices, in the form of investments, to generate future productive capacity and allow our economies to produce more.

'Economists who have studied economic growth have developed theories that aim at answering specific questions about the sources of economic growth by focusing on one type of input at a time. They have developed models that explore how accumulating an input—building the stock of such input—may allow countries to sustain economic growth in the long run.

'What's the key difference between the oven, your skills and the recipe? Try to remember your introductory economics courses. Didn't you distinguish between rival and non-rival goods? Well, then, while the oven and my time are rival inputs (by nature they can't be used simultaneously for multiple ends) the recipe is non-rival! The fact that I'm applying it does not prevent everybody else from cooking the same cake with that same recipe and at the same time! And, more importantly, I don't need to invent it anew from scratch every time I want to cook it! Therefore, when a new idea is created it adds on the stock of existing knowledge and it can benefit society at large!'

'How much does each factor contribute to growth?' one of my classmates asked.

'This is a very important question. The contribution of rival inputs is relatively easy to measure from a quantitative point of view. This is the case because in a market economy the contribution to production is related to the remuneration of such factors, in the form of wages or capital returns. The contribution of non-rival inputs, like the recipe, or more generally of innovation, is harder to measure. This is the case because non-rival inputs lead to externalities. That is, there are side benefits (in the case of innovation) that may not be taken into account in a market economy. To measure the overall contribution of knowledge or ideas to economic growth, economists measure it as a residual, also called the Solow residual.[2] It is the amount of production that cannot be attributed to the use of capital or labour, and it is, therefore, unexplained. It may capture ideas, which improve the way we combine labour and capital, but also other factors that improve how well we work, not how much.'

As the day was coming to an end, and as we finished the lecture, I realised that the professor's class had not only opened a window into the fascinating insight of human and economic revolutions for me, but also into the awareness of our ignorance!

Back home, and as my friends were calling me from the living room to raise their glasses filled with French wine, I remembered how our professor walked us through the different theories of economic growth, explaining how

---

[2]   Solow, R.M. (1956) A contribution to the theory of economic growth, *Quarterly Journal of Economics*, 70, pp. 65–94.

investing in the stock of knowledge, building new ideas, was a source of sustainable long-run growth, contrary to investing in the stock of physical capital, which eventually runs into decreasing returns.

By investing in physical and human capital—education and skills—economies can increase the levels of income per capita. Yet, doing so means fuelling growth by adding more resources. Economists have shown that in the long run these sources of growth cannot sustain growth. Ideas and innovation, on the contrary, *are* a source of sustainable growth, allowing individuals, firms and markets to produce more with less. Keep adding an extra oven into a kitchen with a fixed number of cooks and the same recipe and you will be able to produce more, but each extra oven allows you to produce a smaller additional amount of cakes. On the contrary, ideas and innovation enable us to produce more with the same—or with fewer—inputs and they may be beneficial for the largest number.

But while ideas are non-rival, they do not always freely circulate. Remember my grandfather and his secret recipe! He was trying to make it excludable! Excludability comes from secrecy, but also from rules that try to restrict access, like patents. Then the question becomes: what determines the rate of invention? Patents help protect inventors that put a lot of energy and resources into an uncertain undertaking, boosting the creation of new ideas. But, *ex-post*, once ideas have been discovered, they discourage the sharing and using of these ideas—because they allow the patent holder to sell them at a higher price. This explains why patents are given for a finite duration. But is the stock of knowledge unbound, or is it finite? Is it harder to invent today than it was in the past? How should we price ideas?

'So will you go on any other trips to see old sites?' asked my friend, Jonathan.

'Yes. My dream would be to visit the Areni-1 cave.'

'Where is that?'

'That's in Armenia. A group of researchers from all origins has recently published their findings about chemical evidence for wine production in the cave! An innovation dating back around 4,000 BC!'[3]

'Oh! Fascinating! Now, that was indeed an innovation with lasting effects on society!'

'But do you think it made us better off?' I said.

'Wine, you mean?'

'No — I mean innovation. Comparing the hunter-gathers with us today, some researchers seem to argue that *they* may have been better off. Increasingly intrigued by that question, I decided to call our professor and ask about it…'[4]

'You called her! You should have invited her! So what did she tell you?'

'The agricultural revolution that took place 10,000 years ago led hunter gatherers to abandon their lifestyle in favour of a sedentary life involving the domestication of plants and adoption of agriculture. While the progressivist view holds that human history is about progress, the revisionist view questions this assumption. Based on advances in the study of prehistoric rubbish dumps and of the signs of disease in the remains of ancient peoples — also known as paleopathology — researchers have analysed the health of humans before and after the adoption of agriculture. Revisionists argue that

---

[3]   Barnard, H., *et al.* (2010) Chemical evidence for wine production around 4000 BCE in the Late Chalcolithic Near Eastern highlands, *Journal of Archaeological Science.*

[4]   Diamond, J. (1987) Agriculture: The worst mistake in the history of the human race, *Discover*, [Online], http://tinyurl.com/dl20161210a.

adopting agriculture was detrimental because it decreases diet variety, led to the spread of disease resulting from the crowding out of the population and class division because of the ability to store food. But as others counter-argue, the agricultural revolution did enable a growing population size to be sustained, leading to the difficult question of judging whether society is better off with fewer people who live well, or with lots of people with a lower quality of life. And while crowding out may indeed have made society more vulnerable to disease, it also sparked interactions and innovation itself![5] The creation and sharing of new and of existing ideas may be sparked by settling closer to others. And, because ideas are non-rival, the more they're shared the more benefits for everybody!'

Sharing ideas, I thought to myself… Indeed, human history has been punctuated by revolutions, such as the agricultural revolution, that have been the result of human inventiveness and that have enabled standards of living to increase in per capita terms.

'That's really interesting!' exclaimed Jonathan. 'But the question I ask myself is, will we keep inventing new things in the future?'

'Well, what we know for sure is that recent progress in information and communication technologies do facilitate the sharing of existing ideas at an unprecedented level. Whether the stock of existing ideas will expand forever, or not, depends on your view of the world and of human knowledge. One view holds that the stock of knowledge is limited, and that, as we "discover" parts of it, it becomes

---

[5]　http://www.bradford-delong.com/2016/06/the-worst-mistake-in-the-history-of-the-human-race.html.

harder and harder to invent new and ground-breaking ideas.'

'This is how my sister feels I think: she's doing a PhD in Statistics!' exclaimed Jonathan.

'The other view of the world is that human knowledge is unbound, and that the more we discover the easier it gets to discover new things—as if we were standing on the shoulders of giants. Only the future will reveal which one is true.'

Key concepts

- Solow residual: it is the part of economic growth that cannot be explained by measurable changes in physical capital and labour inputs. It is also called 'the measure of our ignorance' to capture the fact that it measures the unexplained sources of growth.
- Physical capital: machines, equipment and other inputs that constitute a stock used to produce goods through several periods.
- Human capital: education, experience and skills that are embodied in labour and that are used to produce goods through several periods.

Chapter 6

Living together

I surfaced, turned my head to the sky and gulped in a desperate breath of air. I was alive and swimming. I glanced back – the fishing boat had capsized. I prayed that the Tunisian coast guards would show me mercy: me, a European: once comfortable, once the owner of an apartment in Paris, now homeless, now a clandestine trying to escape the events in Europe, and now hoping for a better life in Africa.

In the bookshop, the old professor stopped reading out loud and glanced up at me from the page.

'Now this looks like an interesting book! We're so used to looking at things from our perspective, aren't we? This writer seems to want to provoke us a little and get us thinking about how these poor souls who traverse deserts and seas, war zones and bad harvests, drought and political disputes actually feel. And live through.'

I nodded empathetically and tried to turn my head in such a way as to try to catch the author's name on the spine of the book in my old professor's hands.

'They do that to get to what they think are our rich and pleasant countries', continued the professor, obviously passionate about the subject. 'A better place. They do it in order to obtain a happier, peaceful life. Can we, in the west, or in other developed economies, imagine that? What if those coming to our shores lived in stability and watched on — with varying degrees of comprehension, incomprehension, empathy or anger — as we left our countries and made a bid for freedom, work and safety in *their* countries?'

'And yet', I added, '*we* were just like *them* a century ago. Most of the more than thirty million migrants to the US at the turn of the nineteenth century came from Europe. But clearly, we forgot. And we do not *see* those coming from across the shore. They are invisible to us. Our own history shut down out of comfort.'

As our discussion became more passionate, the bookseller came back and sat next to us, with his coffee in one hand, and a plate of biscuits in the other.

'I couldn't help but listen to what you're discussing. May I join you again? The bookshop's rather quiet today.'

Welcoming him to join us, and taking a biscuit, my professor went on, passionately.

'Today I drove in from the airport. Usually I take the train, but because of the strike I had to drive. As I reached the city exiting from the highway a group of men, women and children were begging for money and holding signs reading *Syrian refugees*. It was really pleasant outside, neither hot nor cold, but no driver had their windows open. Some were ignoring the request by not even looking through the window, maybe thinking to themselves "are they *really* refugees from Syria?" How to know it, if we don't even give them the chance to learn our language, and we don't know theirs. Some drivers, though, were giving them a coin or a cigarette. And through the mechanical stop and go of driving, I realised that the refugees were mostly *invisible* to us.'

'Yes, and sometimes we lack empathy not only for those coming from across the water, but also for our neighbours.

Some clients enter the bookshop and don't even say hello or look at me', added the bookseller.

And the bookseller went on to explain how he found meaning in sharing with his customers' different viewpoints and discussing recent novels or political essays. I then remembered how in the last class of the 'Economic growth' lecture we'd studied the role of a very specific type of capital and which I'd never heard about before: social capital.[1]

'Today, we will study how relations among people are of primary importance for the economy', said the professor. 'More than it may catch the eye at first!'

'Like when you and I chat?' I told Suzanne, whispering.

The ties that we build with others in our communities contribute enormously not only to our individual well-being but also to nourish society's social capital, a key ingredient for economic and social well-being. In fact, many of the exchanges we engage in are with individuals we know little about. Some of these, and many other types of exchanges, require time. That is, they are intertemporal, exchanging resources from today into the future. This means that uncertainty plays an important role in determining the outcome of our exchange with others and/or across time. And as the French writer Marcel Proust so well captured, we live surrounded by individuals, ourselves included, that we think we know, until the day they appear in a different light.[2] And yet, despite all these uncertainties, we trust others, and societies manage to carry those exchanges and prosper. How?

---

[1]   Putnam, R.D. (1995) Bowling alone: America's declining social capital, *Journal of Democracy*, 6 (1), pp. 65–78.

[2]   'Nous vivons auprès d'êtres que nous croyons connaître: il manque l'événement qui les fera apparaître tout à coup autres que nous les savons', Marcel Proust (1913).

'Why do you think we manage to do that?' the professor had asked me.

'Maybe because we get some insurance? Some legal protection?' I'd answered.

'Indeed. We do use insurance and legal rules to protect the parties engaging in an exchange.'

But it is costly to draft and enforce contracts. While for some exchanges we use them, like when we subscribe to a health insurance to cover future health contingencies, or when we buy home insurance, we don't always engage in formal contracting when we exchange with others. And even if we did, we wouldn't be able to perfectly anticipate all the potential events that may happen in the future, or what's also called the *contingencies*. So instead of doing that, we trust others. *Trust*: a key type of capital that can't be touched — it is not physical capital — nor learned in a book — it is not human capital — but it can only be experienced through our exchange with others and it's what constitutes, at the societal level, our social capital. Economists define social capital as the set of beliefs that enable cooperation among members of a community.

Indeed, economic exchange does not occur in a vacuum but requires cooperation among market players. Social capital matters for cooperative exchanges taking place today, especially when the quality of the goods is hard to measure, and over time. We call it *social* because it captures beliefs about others (our trust in others), and it is *capital* because it can be accumulated or eroded. When taking a decision, individuals need to have some prior information about the probability that an event (like, for example, the default of payment from the person that borrowed from us) may happen. When we engage in such a transaction for the first time, there is no personal experience basis for such a prior to be formed. Rather, we rely on social capital, culturally transmitted by our parents, our teachers and our fellow citizens. Our own beliefs and trust in others are the results of the beliefs transmitted to us by our parents (*vertical transmission*), by our teachers (*oblique transmission*) and by our friends (*horizontal transmission*).[3] And as we experience new relations, those experiences and exchanges allow us to update our beliefs. And even if those exchanges are anonymous, if our trading partner is trusted by somebody we know and we ourselves trust, then we're likely to trust them as well.

When we're educated with pessimistic priors about others then we're less likely to trust others and to exchange resources with others. And if we don't engage in new experiences of exchange it's highly likely that our pessimistic priors will reinforce themselves. Why? Because to change our prior we must overcome our pessimism and get to trust and engage in a relationship, hopefully with a positive outcome. Not entering into a relationship doesn't allow us to be surprised.

'So if people don't trust others they're less likely to interact or enter into contact with them, which doesn't allow them to question their opinion about others?' said the bookseller.

'Yes, societies can be trapped into a low trust spiral', said the professor, 'or as economists call it, *low trust equilibrium*, from which it's hard to get out.'

'How hard?'

'It's a difficult question', mused the professor. 'But looking back at history always helps…'

---

3 Bisin, A. & Verdier, T. (2010) The economics of cultural transmission and socialization, in Benhabib, J., Bisin, A. & Jackson, M. (eds.) *Handbook of Social Economics*, Amsterdam: Elsevier.

I was fascinated by the exchange between my old professor and the bookseller, realising that a long-time friendship had been built between them over the years in a subtle and very respectful manner. I just sat there, drinking my coffee and eating, nourishing my body, and listened to them —nourishing my mind.

'You know, economists have traced the persistence of cultural traits to more than 600 years ago, contributing to the spread of violence and hatred throughout centuries...'[4]

'But how can beliefs persist for such a long time? Aren't beliefs individual? Can having violent ancestors make us more violent today? Do you think that how our great grandparents thought influences our way of looking at the world? Is it some sort of hidden inheritance? Then maybe we should tax it!' said the bookseller and the three of us burst into laughter.

'Well, I don't want to spoil the fun,' said the professor after a while, 'but let me give you an example I've come across in my recent readings.'

The bookseller and I were there, captivated and quiet again, listening.

'The Nazi genocide, one of the most extreme and violent historical episodes, was fuelled by German anti-Semitism that has recently been shown to have cultural roots dating back more than 600 years.'[5]

'Really? How did they show it?'

'As it turns out, during the Black Death episode in Germany, Jews were blamed, leading to the pogroms.'

---

[4]   Voigtlaender, N. & Voth, J. (2012) Persecution perpetuated: The medieval origins of anti-Semitic violence in Nazi Germany, *Quarterly Journal of Economics,* 127 (3), pp. 1339–1392.

[5]   *Ibid.*

'But I've heard that Jews vanished from Germany after the fifteenth century and returned during the nineteenth. How can one hate a group or community that isn't even present? How can this hate be transmitted?'

'There are several reasons why this may be the case', intoned the professor. 'Hatred for certain communities may be part of a general mistrust for foreigners or those that are considered dissimilar. In fact, the victims of the Nazi regime were not only Jews, but also—although in smaller numbers—political opponents, homosexuals, individuals with psychological or physical handicaps, or gypsies. Philosophers have studied what fabricates hate, demystifying the idea that hate is natural. And one way that hate fabricates itself is through lack of contact with others. You see, even if the specific target of hate may change, low trust and defiance towards others can be passed on from a generation to the next, and during a political or economic crisis re-emerge with unanticipated strength, taking new forms, in discourse and practical consequences, but perpetuating old attitudes.'

'Yes, but being very close to others may not only be good', I said. 'I remember, when I was a kid, that there was a group of very close friends who were very supportive to each other but who bullied others.'

'Yes, you're right', nodded the professor. 'And I saw that type of thing too when I was young. You see, ties nurtured by strong social capital may also serve coordination purposes for violence and hate because while they contribute to creating a collective identity they may also create *Otherness*.[6] What's critical is the scope at which trust is

---

6 Satyanath, S., Voigtländer, N. & Voth, J. (2017) Bowling for Fascism: Social capital and the rise of the Nazi Party, *Journal of Political Economy*, 125 (2), pp. 478–526.

applied. Our close family and friends network? Or the entire society, regardless of whether we personally know each member of it? The difference between the two is important and economists have extensively discussed how it impacts economic outcomes. It's the difference between *generalised* and *limited* morality.[7] In societies with high "generalised" morality individuals trust others—even those they don't know or they don't necessarily identify with. On the other hand, in societies with "limited" morality, individuals distrust others, except those from their immediate network of family and friends, or those with whom they identify, based on some characteristic—be it ethnic, cultural, linguistic or even religious.'

'So when a society distrusts foreigners, does it mean that generalised morality is low?'

'This is an interesting question, you see. Because the answer really hinges not so much on trust itself, but rather on its scope. In other words, on how widespread it is or on who qualifies as part of an individual's network.'

'So, ideally, if we were to have generalised trust at the global level, we wouldn't distinguish others based on their nationality or their administrative status, would we?'

'Exactly...'

'But what's even more important or interesting is that those communities with whom an individual may identify and trust aren't set in stone', I offered.

'Interesting!' exclaimed the bookseller. 'So the issue isn't so much whether you trust others, or at least not exclusively, but *which* others you do trust. But... trust is based on things

---

[7]   Tabellini, G. (2008) The scope of cooperation: Values and incentives, *Quarterly Journal of Economics*, August; reprinted in: Spolaore, E. (2013) *Culture and Economic Growth, International Library of Critical Writings in Economics*, Cheltenham: Edward Elgar.

like hate and love, no? These are feelings aren't they? Apart from terrible and extreme events, do they *really* matter in our everyday economic lives?'

My professor stood up, stretching her back and, as she did this, I glanced at her, realising that she looked as energised as when she was young.

'Do you remember what a public good is?' she asked me, with a teasing light in her eyes that made me travel many years back into the classroom.

'Public goods... are goods that are non-rival and non-excludable. Their key feature is that even those individuals who do not contribute to finance them may benefit from them. This leads to free-riding behaviour. Think about it! No one would want to finance public lighting because it benefits even those who don't pay a penny for it! In order to increase our contribution to finance public goods we need to trust that others will also contribute, or at least to perceive some benefit in contributing to the well-being of others.

'When we perceive others as being different we may have less empathy for their well-being, decreasing our con-tribution to public goods that benefit both us and them. This is one of the reasons economists point out to explain why communities or countries with high ethnic diversity seem to exhibit lower provision of public goods.[8] Instead, if we come to identify with others, we may be willing to contribute because we internalise some of the benefit of our neighbours and communities.'

'It turns out that when public goods, like schools, are to be provided by diverse communities there will be under-provision. Why?'

[8]   Miguel, E. & Gugerty, M.K. (2005) Ethnic diversity, social sanctions, and public goods in Kenya, *Journal of Public Economics*, 89 (11–12).

'There are several potential reasons why ethnic diversity has been found to be associated with lower provision of public goods. The first one is that when individuals feel apart from others they may participate less in community activities, largely defined. By not getting to know members of other groups they may increase the perceived distance from them. This is aggravated by the fact that people tend to marry those who belong to similar groups or who share similar traits.'

Back in the bookshop, the bookseller crunched on a biscuit and swallowed.

'But can't it just be that individuals belonging to different groups have different tastes and preferences?'

'Sure, that indeed may be the case. Another possibility is that the enforcement of social sanctions associated with anti-social behaviour is harder to achieve between members that identify with different groups.'

'So why not break them apart then and build different schools for different communities?' I said, raising a question for debate.

'Well,' said the bookseller, 'I find that proposal a little short-sighted and static.'

'Static? What do you mean?' asked the professor, raising an eyebrow.

'Well, you know individual tastes today are taken for granted—but in the long run, well, they may evolve depending on who you live with, your group of friends, your broader community, don't you think?'

'Indeed', intoned the professor, glancing across at the plate of biscuits and hesitating to pluck one away. 'Further-more, belonging to a group doesn't mean individuals are isolated from members of other groups. Because individuals may actually identify with several groups at once, depending on which trait is salient at a given point in time and place.

'There's increasing interest in understanding how important an individual's network of relations is in shaping economic opportunities and outcomes, and in influencing individual and entire communities' access to relevant information. Social media networks, but also word of mouth, are important in shaping how we are living together. But measuring the mutual influences between social networks and behaviour and disentangling causality is extremely challenging although not entirely impossible.[9] Moreover, deciding how much to contribute to a public good depends not only on our empathy or identification with the entire community, and to our specific belongings, but also depends on how much information we have about the value of the public good.'

'Well, I know exactly what the value of a square in my neighbourhood is, since this is where I bring my kids to play on Sundays, and I know exactly what benefits the square brings and who uses it', said the bookseller.

'Indeed', nodded the professor. 'But for other public goods we may actually have very little information about their value. Think about public goods related to the environment or to security issues, or even more, to innovation! All of these depend on intertemporal decisions and bear significant amounts of uncertainty. Whether and how we share information within our social networks and communities, therefore, and how these communities are structured,

---

[9] Banerjee, A., Chandrasekhar, A., Duflo, E. & Jackson, M.O. (2018) *Using Gossips to Spread Information: Theory and Evidence from Two Randomized Controlled Trials*, Working Paper revised: March 2018.

becomes essential to how we gather funds, political support and how we implement those public good related decisions.'

'Today this is done through social media, isn't it?'

'Yes, but also through old-fashioned word of mouth. In a world of information overflow it's even more critical to be close to individuals who have reliable information and in whom we trust. A society where communities are isolated and fragmented from each other may have a more difficult time in coordinating the provision of public goods. This is even more the case when public goods require important infrastructure investments and when their scale is large. Now, this doesn't mean that we can't and shouldn't develop special bonds with our family and friends, but rather that how we see, or do not see, ourselves in others shapes our economic and political attitudes. These eventually shape who we are and who we become, individually and collectively.'

'Then we all lose if we stay divided, don't we?'

'Absolutely—a society with lack of trust and a deficit in social capital may be handicapped not only today, but also in the long run.'

The discussion was very intense and I felt in need of a break, when a customer entered the bookshop and the bookseller left us talking. Still, I had questions in my mind, so I asked the professor:

'So, today many people talk about innovation. What's the connection between social capital and innovation?'

'That's an important question indeed. I see you didn't forget how to ask good questions!' she said smiling at me. 'You see, it's especially important to understand the role of networks and of social structure, and how they interact with the spread of ideas. Thanks to network technologies we're more easily connected with others. This can become a tool to build social capital and reinforce social structures.'

'Was your own work affected with the advent of the internet? Did communicating with your co-authors at a distance allow you to be more productive and to stop travelling?' I asked.

'That's, again, a good question', replied the professor, making me blush slightly. 'Well, in answer to your question, I guess it's the same for you at work. I used to travel a bit less, yes. But you know, face-to-face communication remained important at critical moments of the projects I was working on and building trust with my co-authors remained essential. I remember once I had to stay awake for 72 hours in a row to meet a deadline. My co-author and I had online video conferences. The amount of stress was significant as we were under high pressure to meet the deadline. Well, at that moment it was key to have mutual trust—otherwise miscommunication may have ruined our joint effort.'

'That's impressive', I said, smiling, having myself had a few such experiences. 'And I agree entirely—face-to-face remains important.'

'Well, to understand why, one ought to distinguish two key concepts: social capital, on the one hand, and information capital, on the other.[10] While social capital is related to trust—as we've been discussing—information capital is related to shared and open access to information. As has been pointed out, social capital and informational capital are complementary. Indeed, social capital enables society to make better use of informational capital.'

'Hey, sorry, I'm back', said the bookseller, sitting back down next to me.

---

[10] Fountain, J.E. (1998) Social capital: Its relationship to innovation in science and technology, *Science and Public Policy*, 25 (2), pp. 103–115.

'No worries. Did your customer buy something inter-esting?' I asked.

'She was looking for a book about gated communities for her architecture degree', said the bookseller, nonchalantly. 'But I didn't have it, so had to order it.'

'Gated communities? I've heard that phrase,' I said, interested. 'But what are they exactly?'

'Well, they're neighbourhoods that are governed pri-vately — like a club', answered the bookseller.

'An interesting topic!' exclaimed the professor. '*Gated communities*... they're actually closely linked with some of the issues we've discussed. And with environmental sustain-ability issues...'

Key concepts

- Social capital: beliefs that enable cooperation among members of a community.
- Informational capital: information shared by a community.
- Vertical cultural transmission: transmission of cultural traits from parents to their children.
- Horizontal cultural transmission: transmission of cultural traits from peer to peer.
- Oblique cultural transmission: transmission of cultural traits from adults (other than parents, such as teachers) to children.
- Gated communities: neighbourhood that is pri-vately protected through security measures and accessible only to those living in it.
- Generalised morality: norms of good behaviour towards others.
- Limited morality: norms of good behaviour towards members of one's own group.

Chapter 7

The environment

The best things in this life are free, but you can give them to the birds and bees…

As the old professor continued browsing the bookshelves, she began to hum a tune to herself. It was the same tune she had hummed in the lecture hall all those years ago. And it made me smile. We, the students in her class, had kept a respectful silence though we nonetheless sent each other glances that first spoke of surprise, then acknowledgement of her eccentricity, and then puzzlement as she had continued for a full minute. And then total silence. She had looked up from her notes and, peering over her half-moon spectacles, had stared each and every one of us in the face, making us feel quite uneasy, before—much to our astonishment—she suddenly broke into full song.

'*The best things in this life are free, but you can give them to the birds and bees…*'

The effect was that we burst into laughter—perhaps more from relief than humour. But her face had remained calm and passive and once again we turned back into a state of unease mixed with bewilderment.

'It's an old song that has been sung by many', she said at last. 'And perhaps some of you even know it. The Beatles, I remember,' she continued, glancing momentarily out of the window and most probably back to her own childhood, 'sang a version that is perhaps the most famous.' The students nodded. 'But!' went on our professor sharply, suddenly making us start. 'Why do you think I sang this song to you?' Silence. 'Well, let me ask you another question, dear students: *who knows the next line to the song?*'

My student friend Rob raised his hand.

''Cos money, that's what I want.'

'Excellent, Robert', smiled the professor, as an aside commenting that it would have been better if Robert had actually sung it. 'Now, isn't that terrible?' she said, addressing us all.

'In what sense?' said Rob. 'Surely we can't blame people for wanting to make money—after all, that's what makes us do business and fuel the economy, which in turn gives life to our hospitals and roads and—'

'*The music industry!*' I said, making both us and the professor laugh.

The professor held up her hand.

'Correct. But let's return to the first line of the song—it's that part I want you to focus on. Of course we know what the hidden meaning the song writer wants us to understand is. But literally, what are these best things in life that are free? Any ideas?'

'Love', I said, blushing slightly as someone behind me giggled.

'Yes—but that's the metaphor in the song, isn't it', replied the professor. 'Go on. What else?'

'Nothing is free', said another student.

'Really? Go on.'

I raised my hand.

'Air.'

'Good.'

'Grass', said Jennifer, my flatmate at that time.

'Yes! Anything else?' pressed the professor.

'The forests, the sea, the ocean, the clouds, the sunshine, maybe streams, lakes, the footpaths we take when we walk around them.'

'Yes, yes and *yes!*' smiled the professor. 'But *really?* Are these things that we can't grasp or take home with us, that we can feel and experience but can't tangibly pack in a carton—are they really free? And, what's more, are they not goods like any other?'

Once again silence filled the lecture hall. I glanced at Jennifer who glanced back at me. We knew that the professor was technically right, but we didn't know how to argue it. I raised my hand but the professor cut me short.

'It's not so easy, is it, dear students? And there's the conundrum for most people and most economists.' She raised her eyebrows inquiringly as we nodded back in silence. 'So, let's return to that old and magical word *"Love"* that was mentioned at the beginning of this debate. Think about it. Love is something we can take, something we can give and something we can receive. Perhaps we love our parents, perhaps we love our pet cat *Kitty*. We can love the trees, another person, ourselves, chocolate ice-cream or even works of art, books and collecting stamps. But let me tell you a story. It goes like this…'

There was once a heart that was green and lovely. And this heart was in the centre of a land that was pleasant and thriving with all sorts of life. Occasionally, people passed through this land, amazed at the beauty of it all, and took a little bit of that heart and the love it offered. And when they were satiated they thanked the heart and moved on, grateful and looking forward to the prospect that they would return in another six months. Now, there came a time when word got round that the heart was boundless in its capacity to give and make others happy. This, it must be said, was not altogether true—for any heart, as you most probably know, has to have its day off from time to time. Indeed, every heart may also have its moods and surprise us all by suddenly whipping up into anger or deceit. It might create storms, grow barren all of a sudden and give us hardly a drop of what we were expecting, or even decide to close itself off entirely to others for want of rest and time to itself.

But people are funny, aren't they? We create an idea that love is undying and entire—more than entire even. And this idea turned into myths and then beliefs and before we know it that something has become a truth. So, hearing that this beautiful green heart was there to give everything—over and above the norm—people started to think that they could be much happier if they didn't just come and then leave but stay. So little by little, small groups of people settled on the edge of the heart to feed off everything it could offer. And life was so good that they never went hungry. They made new families and grew in number. And because they grew in number they had to demand more from the heart than they usually did and also come up with new ideas.

One such idea was not to hunt the occasional wild beast that lived off the great green heart's generosity, but capture them in number, tame them, and consume them whenever they needed without roaming far afield. So this they did. But, this created a problem. When animals remain wild they move. Once they have eaten their share of luscious grass they leave the place to find another meadow, and thus the grass they ate before grows back in time for when they wander anew into the meadow. However, when all these animals stay in one place, what happens? Of course—the grass doesn't grow back! And this is what happened. And so, ingenious as they were, and observing that their grass hadn't grown back, the people decided to move slightly further into the green heart. And this they did.

It was then that the heart, so generous and so full, decided to become capricious and slightly wary of the ever-demanding people that clamoured for its love. You see, the people, so convinced that their need for love was important, so convinced that love was due, inched further and further, so much so and over so many years that one fine day — in fact a day when the sun in the sky above their heads became exceptionally fierce — they woke up in a sweat to peer outside their dwellings at the terrible sight that met their eyes. The green heart had gone. Left. Disappeared. And a desert of sand had replaced it. A huge desert that today, in our geography and history books, we call the Sahara. Indeed, dear students, if you venture out to this sea of sand one day you'll probably come across the remains of these people's dwellings. And there you'll find, in superb paradox to the endless empty dunes your eyes see before you, engravings on the rocks of all the community that once lived off the love of this once full heart — giraffes, trees, gazelles, elephants, lions, zebras and, of all things, stick people swimming in the heart of the lakes of love that the great heart offered…

The professor looked up, met our silence with a raised eyebrow and said: '*The best things in this life are free, but you can give them to the birds and bees.* Now — what do you think of that?!'

'Well, it bears close resemblance to current environmental issues, and the degradation of common pool resources', said Jennifer, timidly.

'Good! Other ideas?'

'Maybe the tale is not about the heart but about the Earth! In fact, the two words have exactly the same letters — how strange!'

'Well spotted indeed! And of course the tale was a way to introduce our class today, about climate change. Climate change, the greenhouse effect, global warming. Human activity has been identified as a major contributor to the rise in emissions of gases such as CO_2, methane and halocarbons, among others. Climate change is one of the environmental issues that we need to address. But the nature of environmental goods is varied. Importantly, some environmental goods are not really good for us! They are what economists call 'bads'. The difference between a good and a bad is that, while we're willing to pay to consume a good, like a coffee, we're willing to pay *not* to consume a bad! Can you think of an example?'

My mind went back to my first economics lecture, when we were asked what a good was. My inner voice, petulantly, had played with her words—*what is a Good if it isn't Bad?* And here she was, talking of exactly that!

'Waste!' I said.

'Indeed, waste is an environmental bad. But is it rival or non-rival, is it local, or global?' challenged the professor.

'It's rival and local, because if I have the rubbish at home, my neighbours no longer consume it...'

'Exactly. On the contrary, pollution is a non-rival environmental bad. If I pollute the environment I will hurt others and I will contribute to climate change, which has global consequences.'

The professor paused for a moment to contemplate the clouds beyond the window of the lecture hall, almost as if she were asking us to weigh up the importance of the theme of today's lecture. She turned to us. 'A gathering storm or a period of uncertainty before blue skies anew? Food for thought', she intoned, mischievously.

'So let's continue, dear students. Environmental bads that are non-rival lead to negative externalities. A negative externality is a negative side effect that is not considered in the decision-making process of an individual, or a company, and that markets fail to take into account. Think about driving—most of us don't take into account how our CO_2 emissions impact others. And therefore we tend to over-pollute. Collectively we would be better off by changing our behaviour, but none of us has an individual reason, or incentive, to do so. Because outdoor pollution is a non-rival good, markets fail in successfully allocating how much pollution we produce. This is a classic example of what economists call a market failure. How can we solve market failures?[1] And how do economists think about this question?'[2]

'But, professor—without wanting to be provocative, aren't economists mostly focused on studying markets? How can they address environmental problems when such markets don't even exist!'

'Well, then if you think so, you may be surprised today', answered the professor. 'Because economists spend a lot of their time thinking about market failures and how to improve the functioning of markets or the allocation of resources. And so they've also devoted substantial research to studying climate change and environmental issues. Among other topics, they've studied how creating new markets can help decrease atmospheric pollution.'

'But how is that? I mean, to create a market for pollution, someone should own the air. But that's a crazy idea, isn't it?'

'Interesting question! Owning the air… Maybe not that, but can you think about owning the right to pollute? And

---

[1] Kolstad, C.D. (2000) *Environmental Economics*, Oxford: Oxford University Press.

[2] Fullerton, D. & Stavins, R. (1998) How economists see the environment, *Nature*, 395 (1998), pp. 433–434.

would it matter if instead of giving car drivers the right to pollute, we established a right for pedestrians to clean air?'

'It would imply a redistribution of resources from polluters to pedestrians, but it wouldn't change the overall pollution levels if a system of compensation could be established.'

'What do you mean? Explain, please.'

'I mean if car drivers have the right to pollute, then pedestrians could pay them to drive less, to the extent that what they pay rightly compensates car drivers and changes their behaviour. Everyone benefits. And similarly, if pedestrians have the right to clean air, then car drivers could pay them to drive more, to the extent that what they pay rightly compensates pedestrians. Here too, everyone benefits.'

'Isn't this the so-called *Coase Theorem*?[3] And would that work in practice?' said Rob.

'You're absolutely right! Well, it works well under very restrictive conditions... and one of them is that there are no transaction costs!'

'Ah... *transaction costs!* Could you remind us of its definition?'

The professor looked at us with a fleeting air of despair — as though we should have already learnt it off by heart. 'Of course, these are costs associated with engaging in a transaction: searching, gathering information, bargaining a deal, enforcing an agreement.

'One of the ways to address a market failure is to create a market! For instance, creating a market for emission permits. Yet, unless this market is global, it may not fully take into

---

[3]   Coase, R.H. (1960) The problem of social cost, *Journal of Law & Economics*, 3, p. 1.

account negative externalities between countries. No wall can stop air from circulating, no matter how tall such walls are built. Similarly, wildlife, natural habitats and biodiversity know of no political boundaries…

'For instance, we have a market for CO_2 emission permits in Europe.'

'But professor, when I drive I don't pay for it. I mean I don't need to buy any permit.'

'Indeed, the system is only targeting certain industries', replied the professor.

'But why don't we create a global market then?'

'There are several reasons, but one of them is agreeing on how we would distribute the initial amount of permits. Which countries should have a bigger amount of permits? You can easily grasp how politically difficult it would be. The danger would actually be that we give, at the global level, too many permits. If that's the case, then the price of a pollution permit would be too low and would not provide an incentive for firms and citizens to pollute less!

'Solutions to global environmental problems that are addressed at the local level will therefore always fall short. International coordination is then required to deal with them, regardless of the tools (markets, regulation or other mechanisms) used to address them. To coordinate, countries need to agree about how to share the burden of responsibility. Not an easy task! That is, how do we share the burden among the citizens of the world? Should countries be held accountable for the amount of emissions they "produce" today? Should countries be held accountable for the amount of emissions they have ever produced? In other words, because emissions accumulate over time, shouldn't we take into account history? Didn't the countries where the Industrial Revolution started first contribute more to the stock of CO_2?

'Indeed, depending on the approach, who bears the biggest responsibility would look very different! Based on today's emissions China would be among the most responsible countries on Earth!'

'Yes, but isn't its trading partners' consumption responsible for such pollution as well? China exports a big share of what it produces', I offered.

'Interestingly—and in fact, after consumption—much of the waste produced in Europe is exported back to China! And if we take an approach based not on countries but on citizens, then the contribution in per capita terms would be dramatically lower in highly populated countries, like China or India!

'Furthermore, from a strategic perspective, and regardless of who is considered as most responsible for climate change, when states interact with each other, it would be rational for a single country not to cooperate because of the positive externality involved in addressing climate change. That is, individual countries, like individuals themselves, may free-ride and not contribute to finance public goods because of their non-rival nature! So one can quickly understand that dealing with environmental public goods involves both a free-riding problem, because of their non-rival nature, and disagreement regarding how we attribute and measure the responsibility of each country and/or each one of us regarding climate change!

'And yet,' said the professor, 'from a dynamic perspective, countries have to cooperate. And they've tried to cooperate many times in the past! Indeed, dear students, there have been more than 1,000 international environmental agreements!'

'But, professor, are these agreements effective?' I asked. 'Do they help improve environmental outcomes? You said more than a 1,000?'

'Answering your question is really an empirical question. That means that we need to look at the data. One obvious way to address the issue would be to simply compare the outcomes of countries that ratify an agreement with the outcomes of those that don't. But there are two practical problems with this approach. Who can tell me which ones?'

'Well, it may be that the countries that ratify the agreement are different for some other reason that changes how well they perform environmentally. In other words, that the agreement itself is simply a correlate of certain characteristics, but doesn't cause an improvement.'

'This is what we call in economics an omitted variable bias. Are there other reasons why measuring the impact of an agreement is challenging?'

'Well, we don't know what would have happened had the country not ratified the agreement! Maybe the country was already improving, or changing its evolution for other reasons.'

'This is what we call the role of the counterfactual. Simply looking at data may not provide all the answers. These are common problems to most of the empirical work in economics that investigates real country-level data. Another problem, more specific to environmental issues this time, is the fact that for many countries, and for many time periods, especially before the ratification of a given agreement, there is simply no good data available.

'Recently, researchers have studied one specific agreement and setting where they had good data. The agreement is the "Basel Convention on the Control of Transboundary Movements of Hazardous Waste and their Disposal".[4]

'Isn't this related to the fact that countries export their waste to other countries where its disposal is less safe, either because there are no regulations about it or because such regulations are not well enforced?'

'Indeed. Countries engage in what is commonly called "toxic trade", involving trade of hazardous waste, like poisonous waste, etc.'

'But didn't we say that waste disposal is a local issue?' I asked.

'Yes, but it becomes global–due to the fact that countries trade such a waste.'

'Ah! I always thought that trade was bad for the environment anyway', said Angela, a student who always sat at the back of the lecture hall.

'Well,' said the professor, raising her voice to address Angela, 'we'll come back to this issue later. But let's again focus on the Basel agreement. EU countries and other OECD committed themselves to not trading hazardous waste with a group of developing countries. What did the researchers find? As it turns out, the ban did not seem to stop exports of this type of waste!'

'But how did the researchers get the data about toxic trade?' I asked.

'The United Nations has a database, where trade is registered, including different types of waste.'

'So, these agreements don't work?'

4   Kellenberg, D. & Levinson, A. (2014) Waste of effort? International environmental agreements, *Journal of the Association of Environmental and Resource Economists*, 1 (1/2).

'Well, the last word has not been said, but it really seems that the international community will need to rethink how to deal with environmental issues—from local ones such as waste, to global ones such as climate change. Indeed, climate change will require improvements in international cooperation because, as recent estimates point out, massive amounts of people—tens of millions—may be displaced or are already displaced due to environmental factors. They are called "environmental refugees".'

'Why is that?'

'Because global warming may raise the sea-level in many regions of the world, flooding many coastal areas. And because human populations tend to settle near the coasts, this could displace millions.'

'So professor—if people aren't allowed to move and emigrate from their lands, the economic and human costs of global warming will be higher, won't they?'[5]

Our professor looked at us, and before following up on the question walked closer to the lecture hall windows, opening one of them and breathing the fresh air from the park that surrounded our school. The clouds had gone, drifting off towards the north and leaving the day unusually sunny for that time of year. A soft and invigorating breeze entered the class.

'Professor, why don't we finish the lecture outside, in the park?'

It was immediately obvious that she liked the idea. In no time we were all sitting in several concentric rings in the grass surrounding our professor, whose face was half in the shade, half lit by soft sunbeams.

---

[5] Desmet, K. & Rossi-Hansberg, E. (2015) On the spatial economic impact of global warming, *Journal of Urban Economics*, 88 (C), pp. 16–37.

'You see, regardless of which country is *most* responsible for climate change today, the issue we, and especially your generation, will have to think about is how to deal with it.

'There are two ways to deal with climate change. One is to mitigate it, which means reducing carbon emissions and trying to curve the progression of climate change. This can be achieved with international agreements, even if—as experience shows—this may not be sufficient. The other way is to adapt to climate change. As the process of rising sea-levels takes place, the distribution of associated loss and pain will not be equal in all places. In particular, almost half of the population today lives less than an hour's drive from the sea. And even among places that share similar topography, natural catastrophes can lead to very different outcomes. Think about the earthquakes that took place in Haiti and in Chile back in 2010. Climate shocks will affect humanity, but depending on *where* we live the consequences will be more or less strong. So movements of people are likely to be unavoidable, unless we fail politically, and humanly. If people can't move, the costs of climate change are likely to be much higher.'[6]

'But professor, migrating out of one's country is costly isn't it? How will populations affected by environmental changes afford this?'

'You're right to think about that. Some researchers argue that if global warming leads to substantial declines in agricultural productivity by decreasing crops yields, then populations that are already poor may be trapped and unable to finance their emigration.[7] Indeed, such a decrease in crop

6   Desmet, K. & Rossi-Hansberg, E. (2015) On the spatial economic impact of global warming, *Journal of Urban Economics*, 88, pp. 16–37.
7   Cattaneo, C. & Peri, G. (2016) The migration response to increasing temperatures, *Journal of Development Economics*, 122, pp. 127–146.

yields is likely to happen in the tropics. Now, let's go back to Angela's question about trade. As Angela's question transmits, there are many questions and fears regarding whether increasing trade exchanges, not only of toxic waste but in general, leads to higher pollution. This touches on the bigger question of what determines pollution. Let's start thinking about the broader question.

'Economists have studied the question and found that pollution depends broadly speaking on three major factors: the scale of economic activity—that is, how much a country produces—the composition of economic activity—what type of goods a country produces—and lastly technology—that is, how efficiently the goods are produced. Changes in pollution, therefore, can be traced to each of these different factors. Interestingly, and here is where trade comes into the picture, the composition of production may vary over time in a given country because there are changes in consumer habits and demand, and/or because the country specialises in producing certain goods and imports the rest from foreign countries.'

'Professor, does this mean that countries that don't seem to pollute much but that import many goods produced in a highly polluting way are, from a consumption perspective, really contributing to increasing the stock of CO_2 emissions?'

'Yes, this can indeed happen. One of the reasons for the displacement of pollution is surely the result of different environmental regulations across countries and what economists call the "pollution havens hypothesis", according to which countries with stringent regulations delocalise their production to those with weaker strings attached. So has it happened? Is there evidence supporting this hypothesis?

'One interesting period researchers have looked into is 1990s trade liberalisation. To measure the composition effect, and test the pollution haven hypothesis, economists measure the pollution content of exports relative to that of imports. Interestingly, researchers have found that from 1990 to 2000 the pollution content of Chinese exports, relative to their imports, seem to have declined.'[8]

One of my classmates, Joyce, raised her hand. I knew her little, because she was working on creating her start-up company in the solar panel industry and she had little time to hang out after class. We all moved a little to listen to her, as we expected she would share some of her insights about the industry.

'The idea that there's a race to the bottom in environmental regulation — that is, that countries will compete to attract factories at the cost of increasing pollution — is too binary anyway.'

'That may be the case, Joyce', granted the professor. 'Would you like to share some of your insights from your ongoing project? I'm sure everyone would love to learn more about it.'

I had always liked that about our professor — her ability to recognise when someone in the class, or more broadly in the school, had interesting insights about an issue and her willingness to learn from it.

'Sure', replied Joyce. 'Thanks. Well, as some of you know, I've been working in the solar panel industry for a couple of years now. And the case of solar panels is quite interesting in undoing some of the stereotypes that we may have about developed and developing countries' stances regarding the environment. In fact, the European Union and the US have been having disputes with China over solar power

---

[8]   Grether, J.-M., Mathys, N.A. & de Melo, J. (2010b) Unravelling the worldwide pollution haven effect, *Journal of International Trade and Economic Development*, iFirst, pp. 1–32.

technology. It turns out that the Chinese are more efficient at producing solar panels! Westerners, instead of thanking them, have pushed for protectionist measures, but this makes no sense at all!'[9]

'Well, but I can understand they are trying to protect their own industry', said Angela, from the back.

'But as it turns out,' continued Joyce, 'while the Chinese are more efficient at producing solar panels, westerners are more efficient at producing polysilicon, which serves as an input used in the production of solar panels!'

'Isn't that what you are working on?'

'Yes, exactly.'

'Thanks Joyce for your interesting insights', intervened the professor. 'Indeed, it shows us how developing cleaner and greener technologies to mitigate climate change requires us to trade and cooperate with others. And it may not be a zero-sum game. It also requires us to go beyond pre-conceived ideas about the role of trade and how economic activity impacts pollution.'

'Are there other important factors to consider?' I asked.

'What about the climate change sceptics? Should we consider their beliefs and potential influence on others?' said Rob.

'This is a key issue to consider, Rob, because costly action to deal with climate change today, even if leading to future benefits, needs to be perceived as acceptable. This replies to the more general question about how individual and collective attitudes towards the environment and towards climate change can vary greatly by country. And how these attitudes

---

9   Frankel (2013) Protectionist clouds darken sunny forecast for solar power, *VOX, CEPR's Policy Portal*, [Online], https://voxeu.org/article/protectionist-clouds-darken-sunny-forecast-solar-power.

are channelled into the traditional political spectrum is rather important. So, to sum up,' said the professor, smiling and obviously concerned that we might be a little tired after taking in so much interesting information, 'environmental issues can be dealt with locally, nationally and on a global scale. Being in favour of preserving the environment doesn't necessarily require favouring local, national or international intervention and it, most likely, involves all of these levels of action. It all depends on the nature of these environmental goods. Now, enjoy your well-earned break, dear students!'

Key concepts

- Environmental good: a good that is related to the environment and that has a positive value or impact, such as clean air, clean water, etc.
- Environmental bad: a good that is related to the environment and that has a negative value or impact, such as pollution, waste, etc.
- Pollution haven hypothesis: hypothesis according to which companies choose to locate in countries with weak environmental regulations to reduce their costs.

Chapter 8

Anti-globalisation

Here Smith was – confronted with a bigger picture, a bigger truth, and where Smith's whole set of beliefs was put at risk...

This time, it was I who, leaving the old professor in her thoughts and browsing, wandered among the bookshelves of the quaint shop. At one point, letting my instincts pull me towards a row of book spines, I bent down, hovered, closed my eyes and plucked a book from its nest among the others. I studied the cover, convinced that, unlike the old adage, one could indeed judge a book by its cover. Not too bad, I concluded, acknowledging the art work. And then, of course, the blurb on the back cover—the domain of the marketers and a sure binary trigger to decide whether or not to open the book and read a few lines. Hmm, interesting... Baited, teased, enticed and wholly aware of it, I decided to open the book and browse a few lines. The copywriter had done a very good job. And I was ensnared.

'There was once a scientist called Smith. And Smith had a burning ambition. Smith, let's not give the person a gender or first name—for (s)he could be any one of us—' went the intriguing opening lines to the story, 'wanted to prove that there was intelligence in a fish scale. Now, it could well be that Smith's burning ambition had been born from the fact that Smith had grown up by the sea and had often watched the trawlers come back from their long and arduous voyage to disembowel their hulls of silvery cod and herring. It could also have been due to the fact that as a child Smith had been enchanted by the sight of a gift shop window on the seafront that sported a singing fish—the type that writhed and waggled its tail as it sang some silly tune. Smith—secretly, for (s)he had never admitted it—had stayed for hours in front of that shop window mesmerised by the jaunty fish that sang the old English sea shanty *Bobby Shaftoe*.

'Now Smith had grown up wanting to be a sailor and by the age of eight Smith had joined the local boat club to learn the basics. But it was not to be. Poor Smith discovered, much to his/her chagrin, that the moment the little sail boat set out to sea, sea-sickness set in. Any voyage, however great or small, was doomed to misery and a very green and desperately ill Smith. Now Smith wasn't one to just give up. There are, after all, many paths to one's dream. So, discovering that (s)he had an aptitude for studies and in particular maths, science and biology, Smith rapidly understood that a scientific life would allow the sea-dream to be reached.

'And here Smith was. Aged thirty-one, PhD, a successful marine biologist, member of the National Marine Scientific Committee, an acclaimed researcher on mollusc diversity in the eastern Atlantic and holder of a burning ambition: to prove that there was intelligence in a single fish scale.

'Now, Smith spent many hours during and after work peering at thousands of fish scales through the microscope. Indeed, the powerful microscope magnified a single scale to human-like proportions and beyond. They were beautiful. Sumptuous. Works of art on a scale—if that is the word to use—of Gustav Klimt, Isaac van Duynen or the modernist painter John White. Altogether, Smith and the microscope had a very close up view of what intelligence might be. And

Smith was so preoccupied with the micro-world revealed through the eyepiece and the rainbow-coloured scales splayed on the glass plate that (s)he became convinced that the truth lay in that single vision of things. Many nights and much concentration were given to searching for the answer to that burning ambition and it was all very tiring.

'And after a year of exhausting analysis, on the verge of giving up, one night Smith yawned, stretched and withdrew from a hunched position over the microscope. And suddenly, a strange vision came to Smith. In fact, more of a view than a vision. Not only was Smith looking at the microscope that was peering at the fish scale, Smith could see the whole fish lying on a plate next to the scientific instrument — the entire thirty centimetres of creature — scales, mouth, head, eyes, gills, fins, spine and tail. If extracted from the view from the microscope it was an enormous ensemble of a creature, a powerful being. And maybe, Smith's mind hesitated, a whole intelligence in itself! *Oh no!* Suddenly, Smith felt oddly fearful. And strangely very small. Here Smith was, confronted with a bigger picture, a bigger truth, and where Smith's whole set of beliefs was suddenly put at risk. A voice inside Smith said, "*but this is too big and scary!*" Another voice raised itself to cry, "*but it's different and foreign to what I've always thought was true!*" And yet another chimed, "*If this picture invades my own, then I'll be forever doomed to second place!*" The moral of the story of Smith the scientist? It is that the bigger picture is always scary at first sight. And that whatever the resistance we cry aloud, we know deep inside that we are, like the fish, part of the same big ocean of things. And that, my dear readers, is very scary indeed.'

Superb! I said inwardly, and no sooner had I decided to purchase the very book that the noise of a distant clamour came from outside the shop. I turned my head, craned my neck — and caught both the bookseller's and the professor's eyes. They too were intrigued. The noise came closer and closer, obviously a gathering of people, and soon we were able to make out the cries and hoots and shouts. It was a demonstration and before the bookseller could gather in his special offers stand from the pavement outside, the great serpent of demonstrators was upon us. *No, no, no!* came the nasal chant from a megaphone, taken up by the hundreds of voices in the crowd — *No, no, no! Glob-alisation's got to go!*

'Oh, anti-globalisation! Such a buzz word!' said the bookseller, shaking his head.

'One may say so, indeed', hummed the professor. 'Actually, I had the same feeling, and I recently checked the use of the word online in existing corpus. As it turns out, its use has exploded in recent years!'

Taking advantage of having the professor's attention, I couldn't resist asking her: 'Why is that? And how would you define anti-globalisation?'

'Well,' said the professor, staring steadily through the window as though speaking to the demonstrators, 'there can be many different ways of defining it. But I would say that anti-globalisation is a general scepticism about trade and its benefits, as well as an anti-immigration sentiment, which together would call for closing borders.

'Brexit has been one of the manifestations of the rejection of globalisation, or of anti-globalisation backlash, of recent years. This rejection draws from the sentiment that migration has had negative consequences, in both economic and social terms, for the UK economy. These consequences include, the argument goes, a deterioration of labour market outcomes for low-skilled workers, which is based on the assumption that immigrants are susceptible to replace native workers, especially low-skilled and young ones. Studies starting back at the turn of the century have investigated this hypothesis in the data. While most of the studies are based on US data, there has been an increased interest in the UK experience since the mid-2000s. These studies show that these potentially negative effects are not supported by the data, neither in the short run nor in the longer run.[1] Migrants are not replacing or taking jobs from native British people, simply because the amount of jobs available at any point in time is not fixed! Another concern that's often voiced is that migrants push wages down because of the increase in the labour supply, making labour more abundant. Regarding wages, studies that find a negative impact do so only for the very bottom of the distribution and for very small amounts! But migrants do, however, have a positive effect on average wages. In fact, other factors seem to be more important in shaping the evolution of wages—such as technology, for instance.

'It's entirely possible, therefore, that negative stereotypes shaped by the public debate make migrants become the scapegoat for those who lose their jobs, and for the politicians who propose closing borders as a solution to problems that, if anything, have other roots.

'Furthermore, immigrants to the UK include both low-skilled and high-skilled workers! But high-skilled migrants are often called "expatriates", aren't they? So isn't that preventing a balanced political debate, with a more nuanced and realistic description of *who* migrants really are in their diversity of origins, skills, backgrounds and in their potential contribution to the economy?

'Another argument against migration is that it decreases how productive a country is. By increasing the labour

---

[1]   Portes, J. (2018) *The Economic Impacts of Immigration to the UK*, [Online], www.voxeu.org.

supply, it would, the argument goes, decrease the invest-
ment in capital inputs in favour of hiring low-skilled and
cheap labour. But this argument doesn't take into account
that migration has an impact on the decisions and behaviour
of native workers! Think about communication skills for
instance. Native workers, even for the same skill level, have
an advantage in tasks that require intensive communication.
This may provide incentives for native workers to specialise
in those tasks, making them complementary, not substitutes,
to migrants' labour and skills. Similarly, native workers may
train themselves more, as a response to the inflow of
migrants. So at the individual level migrants may contribute
to the questioning of a status quo, pushing individuals to
upgrade their skills and consciously shape their careers.
Immigration may, therefore, be a positive force.[2] Moreover,
studies have found a positive correlation between migration
and productivity.[3]

'While establishing causality, especially at the country or
cross-country level, is particularly challenging (in other
words, immigrants may choose to settle in high performing
countries), the evidence seems to suggest that they do not
replace natives, that they may boost natives' acquisition of
human capital and that they themselves may bring skills and
knowledge to a country. Furthermore, most migrants are
young working-age adults that have been at school in their
country of origin. While their impact on fiscal resources
needs to be thought about using a longer time horizon, the
fact that they arrive at working age means that their fiscal
contribution in the short run is likely to be positive. Yet, in a

---

[2]   Peri, G. & Sparber, C. (2009) Task specialization, immigration, and
        wages, *American Economic Journal: Applied Economics*, 1 (3), pp. 135–169.
[3]   Peri, G. (2012) The effect of immigration on productivity: Evidence from
        US states, *Review of Economics and Statistics*, 94 (1), pp. 348–358.

context of budget austerity, this contribution has remained invisible to the public opinion, or even worse, the latter has been blamed on them!

'By closing borders and decreasing migration flows, from both low and highly skilled workers, a society has much more to lose that meets the eye. Not only because of the direct contribution of migrants to the labour market and to the fiscal position of a country, but also because they seem to spark specialisation and further accumulation of human capital.

'In the words used by the press, and in the conversation of daily life, migration flows are often described metaphorically as "migration waves". This image is not specifically used in English-speaking countries, but also in French-speaking countries (*la vague migratoire*), and in Spanish-speaking countries (*la ola migratoria*), etc... Using a wave as an image is not neutral. It suggests that the flow is of an unstoppable force and that it crashes to the shore and submerges everything in its passage. But this image gives very little credit to the native populations themselves. Data show that native populations are not passively waiting on the seashore, but rather that they are themselves in flux and movement, maybe not from abroad, but within: changing jobs, training and acquiring new skills or specialising in new tasks, entering the labour force, creating jobs — in short, changing their behaviour in a number of ways that give us a different story about migration flows. Not as a scary and brutal wave, but rather as increasing the diversity of the river delta's assemblages.

'More importantly, the image also seems to suggest or convey the idea that migrants arrive in a "natural" way, while they are instead more likely to get themselves sunk by a real wave in the Mediterranean before they can even get to the shore.'

'But professor,' said the bookseller, frowning, 'anti-globalisation movements and political parties reject not only inward migration but also trade.'

'You're right. The idea is that by opening borders and trading with the rest of the world a country may win—through its exports, some domestic industries may gain access to bigger markets—but also lose—because some jobs get lost in favour of importing goods that were previously produced within its borders. Those segments of the population that were employed in the industries that become outpaced by foreign companies could, *a priori*, reject globalisation.[4] A recent study has actually studied political stances in German regions that have industries that win, or lose, from trade.'[5]

'Why study Germany? It didn't leave the EU, at least not yet', said the bookseller, laughing.

'True, but German trade increased significantly with China and with Eastern Europe after the fall of the Iron Curtain', replied the professor. 'Let me explain.

'There has been a rise in electoral support for far right anti-globalisation parties in Germany. Interestingly, the regions where imports have increased the most are those where support for far-right parties have seen the strongest progress, while the opposite seems to be the case in exporting regions. A key question to think about is to what extent politicians are simply responding to an increasingly anti-globalisation demand. In other words, do they capture such

---

[4]   This argument, though, misses the fact that individual workers, regardless of where they work, are also consumers and that trade actually leads to both price and quality improvements, as well as a higher diversity of goods available.

[5]   Dippel, C., Gold, R. & Heblich, S. (2015) Globalization and its (dis-) content: Trade shocks and voting behaviour, *NBER working paper #21812*.

a vote? Or are they constructing this sentiment thanks to certain rhetoric and language based on the observation that trade patterns have evolved? And yet, we do not know what the counterfactual would be. That is, what would have happened to employment, wages, prices, etc. if trade had not increased in Germany?

'Much of the political and economic debate surrounding anti-globalisation is about its distributional consequences — about discussing *who* wins and *who* loses from trade openness and migration inflows. And from a policy perspective governments and political parties discuss how to act on it. That is, how to compensate the losers.'

'Yes, but Europe isn't doing anything on the social front!'

'Well, maybe not nothing. Maybe it's just that you didn't hear about it! But Europe has set up a fund to compensate the so-called "losers" of globalisation.'

'Really? What does it do? I've never heard of it. What's it called by the way?'

'The European Globalisation Adjustment Fund.[6] In the US there is a similar institution, called the Trade Adjustment Assistance.

'The European Globalisation Adjustment Fund was created in 2007, just before the great recession. This fund partners with EU countries to train workers that have lost their jobs because of globalisation. In practice, the great recession that came right after its creation has meant that a big share of the funding has gone to finance training for workers that were affected *not* by globalisation but by the *crisis*. Indeed, during recessions trade collapses, usually by a

6   Claeys, G. & Sapir, A. (2018) The European Globalisation Adjustment Fund: Easing the pain from trade?, *Bruegel Policy Contribution No 2018/5*.

bigger order of magnitude than economic activity.[7] Some researchers actually argue that the great recession led to xenophobic reactions with respect to migrants.'

'But, dear professor, I remember a much more optimistic view of the world a few years ago. We used to discuss the changes in global poverty and inequality. What happened to that?' I said.

'You're right! Reality has not fundamentally changed, and the world did experience a spectacular decline in poverty and in inequality at global levels! Think only of the progress that China and India have made—and these are among the most populated nations in the world! Many regions of these countries went from darkness to light, as the satellite data show. In western countries we may forget what a privilege and luxury it is to be able to read at night, to be able to work or write even when the sky is dark and our bodies are tired. Our minds can daydream at the latest hour. Well, this is progress that has happened worldwide.'

'So, is it just that we forget this evidence? Why has the consensus that globalisation was a good force led to the existing debates and rise of anti-globalisation? Why do some people hold very negative views on globalisation then?'

'Some researchers', replied the professor, returning to watching the last of the demonstrators walk past the bookshop window, 'have actually pointed out some of the existing biases in the way the issue of anti-globalisation is

---

[7]   Out of the 132 million euros spent in 2010, only 17 million were spent on training services for workers that were negatively affected by globalisation.

framed.[8] Not only in political discourse but also in economics research.'

'What biases exactly?'

'Well, the first bias is that a lot of the existing analysis is static. That is, it focuses on short-term impact without taking into consideration the behavioural responses of native populations to changing trade and migration flows.'

'But, professor, didn't we see that our habits today are greatly determined by our former trading relations? Without trade there wouldn't be any pizza from Naples, you see!'

'Exactly! So arguments that focus on static costs and benefits are missing a big part of the story.[9] Movements of goods and people, and for that matter of capital, change the economy first because they change the scale of it. But remember, when we invent a new idea, the bigger the number of individuals that can benefit from it the better. Non-rival inputs that can be used simultaneously by different people and in different places tell us that when the size of the market is bigger, the benefits of such inventions can be enormous. Some economists have used this to explain why rock stars or football players earn increasingly extravagant sums of money. Why? Because their reach is global!'

I smiled at the old professor. She hadn't lost an ounce of her vitality and passion for debate.

'It makes me think', she continued, 'of an encounter I experienced. Sitting in a café in Paris, I began a casual conversation with my neighbour at the next table. We started talking about our jobs. His was to work at the service of very rich people, planning their parties and trips. As he explained

8   Desmet, K., Nagy, D. & Rossi-Hansberg, E. (2016) The geography of development, *Journal of Political Economy*, and *CEPR Discussion Paper 10544*.

9   *Ibid.*

the ins and outs of his profession, he gave me a recipe for success: if you manage to sell one baguette to each French citizen at one euro each, you earn more the 60 million euros!

'What was true about the French baguette is even more true of current innovation. Why? Because innovation today requires scale, as it's often characterised by network technologies. In other words, these are innovations or technologies whose value increases with the size of the network. By focusing on the short-term in the calculation of the costs and benefits of globalisation, rather than taking a longer term perspective, anti-globalisation analysis may miss important benefits from openness that do not materialise immediately but that result from the increasing size of markets.

'The anti-immigration stance is also suffering from a short-term approach.[10] Indeed, it is plausible that in the very short-term migrants can increase congestion in access to certain types of infrastructures and services. But this misses entirely a consideration of the fact that the size of the pie (economic output) is not fixed. And that migrants may contribute positively to make it bigger. How? By increasing the labour force, by bringing new ideas and skills, by increasing the demand of goods and services.'

'But professor, aren't these similar arguments to those used to bring women into the labour force?'

'Indeed. By increasing the female labour force participation, markets become bigger—a scale effect—and the allocation of resources becomes more efficient—untapped potential is revealed. The second bias of much of the current work that has also been pointed out by research is the fact

10   Desmet, K., Nagy, D. & Rossi-Hansberg, E. (2016) The geography of development, *Journal of Political Economy*, and *CEPR Discussion Paper 10544*.

that a lot of the existing analysis is what economists call *partial equilibrium*. That is, it fails to take into account the interactions between different markets. In particular, there is a relation between the flow of goods, the flow of people and the flow of ideas, and—*in fine*—the rising of prosperity across borders. In economics, partial equilibrium means that the authors study only one market, without considering feedback effects and changes operating in other markets as a consequence. When economists study the interaction of markets together, they do what they call *general equilibrium*. But in reality, as we previously discussed, the arrival of migrants in one industry, region or even neighbourhood will have further consequences and where the host society evolves and adapts as well.'

'Maybe this is what scares many people? Change they don't want to experience?'

'Probably part of it is related to this resistance, yes', said the professor, turning back to the plate of biscuits to realise that there were none left. 'And to the view that identity, both at the individual level and at the collective level, is something fixed. But it isn't. It evolves. I remember my grand-mother saying to me: *I'll never go back to visit my country of origin.*'

'Why?'

'Well, she said: *I'm sure things have changed so much I wouldn't recognise it.*'

'Maybe what we are attached to are the memories of our younger selves', I suggested. 'And while these memories are important and precious, we also accept that our individual lives and identities evolve. So, why is what's true about our own selves not applied to the idea we have of our countries? So much of the debate argues about whether immigrants assimilate to the local culture. But we may wonder whether the local culture also adapts to the immigrants. It goes both ways.'

'Why don't we see that?' said the bookseller. 'Are we all blind, seeing only part of a bigger whole?'

'Maybe societies are attached to their culture?' I added.

The old professor held up a hand, much as she used to do in class—a sign for the debate to come to a halt.

'Economists have recognised that culture plays an important role in economic exchange. Could it be a reason why societies, beyond individuals, are attached to it?'

The old professor glanced at the clock on the wall above the counter and sighed. It was time to go. She looked at me and shrugged her shoulders.

'It was such an unexpected and enchanting meeting, my dear', she said softly and, if I was not mistaken, a little embarrassed. 'You must come and visit me—and soon.'

'The years go by so quickly', I offered, though wanting to say so much more. 'Yes, we must meet again soon. *I promise.*'

We remained silent for a few moments and then she gave a little nod of her head.

'And I see you're going to buy that book.'

'Yes. Yes, I think I will.'

'A good choice', she whispered, sending the bookseller a knowing glance. 'Well—I must go. I've got a plane to catch myself. Bye, Thomas.' She shook the bookseller's hand, leant across to give me a kiss on the cheek and then turned towards the door and the street beyond. 'Oh!' she said, now a silhouette standing in the open doorway. 'I've an idea. If you have the time and means, why not come and visit me in Valparaiso? Now *that* would be a place that would change your outlook on things, I can tell you! Take care, my dear.'

'Farewell, dear professor', I called after her, and she was gone.

The bookshop seemed suddenly very empty now, although, in reality, the old professor's presence and smell — the faint scent of her perfume spiced with lemon — still lingered. I looked, not without a hint of sadness, at the bookseller and handed over the book.

'And the train ticket?' I said, looking the bookseller in the eye as I paid for the book and placed it in my bag.

'Ah, that…' he said, and a little smile came to his lips. He picked it up from the counter where I had placed it and studied it. 'Hmm, it certainly sounds like an adventure', he mused. 'Did you notice the name of the destination?'

I nodded.

'Well, as far as I'm concerned,' he said, handing it to me, 'if someone left it there, then it was meant for you to find it.'

I shook my head, unsure of whether I would actually use it. Maybe, I thought, I could randomly give it to someone in the street on the way back home. Like this, it would be someone else's destiny.

And now, noticing my hesitation, it was the bookseller's turn to shake his head. He looked up and met my gaze. Smiled.

'Have courage. Take the train. And maybe', he added, with an air of mischief, 'you'll write a book about it all!'

Chapter 9

A way forward
Taking the train ticket

When you journey to another land, a stranger in a strange land you may be. What do you call yourself? And what do others call you? An adventurer, a foreigner, a migrant, an explorer, an alien, a tourist, a guest, a traveller, an immigrant, a visitor, an expatriate, a burden, a bringer of wealth? Maybe all or more of these, but maybe you would refute some of them. Remember, dear travellers, call others by the name that you would call yourself when in a strange land.

The old professor was still in my mind when, one week later, with a day taken off work, I set out to board the train that would take me to Enfer. *I like train journeys*, I said inwardly, thinking that perhaps we too easily opt for our cars. I watched the tall buildings and towers of the big city trail behind and then they were gone, replaced by the sprawl of suburbia, neatly lined streets, trees, schools and parks. This was where the young families lived, couples commuting to their jobs in the day and returning to pick up their children from schools and childminders. It passed through my mind that perhaps I, in some near future, would fit into this picture of things. And one day, at the end of my career, with the birds in the family having flown the nest, I would leave

to live a new life in another country—just like the old professor. Thirty minutes later and the countryside entered my
gaze as if a curtain had been drawn between suburbia and I.
It was all so sudden that my mind, turning practical, wondered if the region the train had just entered was protected
in some way—a nature reserve or national park or something. Field upon field upon field gave way to gentle valleys
and little villages, open skies and horizons cluttered only by
trees and forests. And I was still an hour and half from my
destination!

As I sat—and this was true whenever I took a train or a
plane—I felt the fleeting fantasy of randomly meeting 'the
one' next to me. Maybe, in my subconscious, or my story, I
knew I was the fruit of a train journey and the encounter
between my grandparents in Alger.

That day, though, it was not love or friendship that was
sitting next to me but rather debate as a fellow passenger
came walking up the aisle between the seats, looking for a
spare seat. He hesitated in front of me, looked inquiringly
and, when I nodded that the seat opposite was free, sat
down with a sigh. When I think back, maybe love and
friendship are about debate as well. Being able to exchange
views in a respectful manner, with one another.

'I've walked up most of this train', he said, wiping his
brow. 'I'd never have thought so many people would want
to go to the countryside!'

I smiled, a sign that I too had been surprised. But apart
from this, at first glance it seemed my fellow passenger and I
had nothing in common—except perhaps, as I discovered
later, an interest in the news and a taste for debate.

I returned to gazing out of the window, and finally
decided to open my newspaper for a little distraction and—
to tell the truth—something to indicate to him that I was
occupied. I browsed the front page with its headlines, flicked

through a few pages and came across an article that seemed interesting.

Paris, Thursday April 19th 2018, it read, written by someone going under the name of Janice Highgrove, special reporter:

'Place de la République, on an unusually warm day for this time of the year with a blue and clear sky. Movements of people, walking, biking or running, animate the large square. Some are going to work or to study, some are just enjoying the sun and the breeze. The Place de la République is an open space, with the statue presiding in the middle, often the place for gatherings of varied circumstances, happy and sad, mixing crowds, old, young, from all walks of life, that mingle together in a never-static fashion. Located strategically, it attracts people from popular Belleville in the north, from the trendy Marais in the south, from effervescent Bastille in the east and from the Porte St Martin in the west. There is only one café in the square, named after the motto of Paris: Fluctuat Nec Mergitur.'

Enjoying this quiet and warm moment, feeling the chunk-chunk of the train as it sped onwards into the countryside, my phone suddenly vibrated in my bag. The number showing up was unknown and foreign, but I decided to answer:

'*Oui bonjour?*'

'Hi Stephanie! This is Martha, your old professor calling.'

'Ah Martha! It's so nice to hear from you again. Have you changed your phone number?'

'Well, you might say I have. I'm calling you from Valparaiso, Chile. I'm settling in the house my uncle Henri left to me, do you remember?'

'That must explain the sound', I said, rather loudly, conscious that my fellow passenger was looking at me with a frown. 'The line's a little crackly from time to time.'

'You can save it if you want', I heard her say. 'We'll keep a line in London but will spend little time there from now on.'

'Sounds great. I'll keep that in mind.'

The old professor started to discuss recent economic and political events and I could feel she hadn't lost an ounce of energy and curiosity about the world. The most recent event she mentioned was the result of the elections in Hungary and the rise of anti-globalisation voting, not only in Hungary but among parts of the electorate in many countries. At one moment, the phone cut out, came on clear again, and then began crackling repeatedly.

'Time to hang up, I'm afraid', I said. 'Time to hang up, Martha.'

'Well dear, it's nice talking with you, as always', I heard her voice, faint now. 'And I really encourage you to write that book. What was its title again?'

'*The nature of goods and the goods of nature.*'

'Sounds good. And don't forget to keep me updated — and let me know when you have a first draft! And also don't forget that you're welcome anytime in Chile!'

We said our goodbyes and I smiled apologetically to the passenger opposite who had since opened his own newspaper and was pretending, with much concentration and a furrowed brow, to read. I decided to go back to my article myself.

'As I finish my coffee I walk towards the crowd and distinguish people wearing blue t-shirts, the organisers. Someone next to me asks one of the organisers what is going on. "We are organising this for homeless and migrants, providing them with food and basic hygiene products." But something bothers me. I ask the organiser: why do you have these barriers?

I see the homeless and migrants, mostly young men, huddle behind a small access between two metal barriers. They are allowed to enter individually and very slowly, after two security guards check their bags and their pockets. Once inside, they are directed to different stands by the volunteers. All around the perimeter, people stop and look inside, as if there were something to see. A music band is playing, the volunteers are chatting among themselves, and the space is mostly empty. At most ten people are gathering at the entry point waiting to be screened. It is midday. I walk towards the entry point, and ask another organiser:

"Why do you have these security fences?"

"We have to – we have no choice."

"But for what reason?"

"For security reasons", replied the organiser. "Some of them come with arms, or are drunk."

Another organiser comes close to me. He engages in an open discussion.

"This isn't true. Last year the same event took place in Porte de la Chapelle, without any gates or fences."

I look around and nobody seems to be either drunk or violent. Plus, these barriers are not bulletproof anyway. I keep arguing with the head of the organisation who is uncomfortable with my questions and my presence and eventually stops talking to me:

"Either you want to enter and help us, or stop this argument!"

I know that the organisers are good-hearted, that they want to help the homeless and the migrants. But I think they are unconscious about the fact that screening them, and gating the gathering, may stigmatise these individuals even more. I leave the square, which now looks divided and partly gated, under the deep blue sky, wondering why we treat homeless and migrant individuals, who in any case live on the streets, as dangerous while we try to help them, exactly on the streets and squares where they usually live.

And I realise that even those that are supposed to welcome and help migrant populations hold well-anchored stereotypes *associating migrants with violence, addiction and other anti-social behaviour.*[1]

And this image of the Place de la République with the gated migrants with this association sticks in my mind. I feel it is an image of the broader drama that is going on today in our borders. Our gated countries, where fences are deeply ingrained, not only in our lands and coasts but also and most critically in our minds.'

I closed my newspaper carefully and placed it down on my lap. Glancing back from the passing countryside, my gaze caught that of my fellow passenger who had also placed his newspaper aside. I suddenly got the feeling that he wanted to talk to me.

'I love how she highlights what we don't see.'

'Excuse me?' I said.

'Yes, the journalist, Highgrove. I saw you were reading her article too. It's quite poignant how she places us in that very moment. It reminds me of my own experience in my district in Paris back in 2015.'

'Well, maybe, but she can't come up with a single proposal, you see!'

'True. But you know these are issues that we can't solve with a set of "ten things to do every day". No quick fixes!'

'So what would *you* propose? I mean how would you address the rise of anti-globalisation?'

Thus it was that my fellow passenger and I embarked on the train of conversation. I took a deep breath and gazed through the window once again. We were now traversing hills and the sun was still up, warming the window and my left arm. I suddenly felt that going to Enfer was the right thing to do, soon to discover that what ended up enchanting

---

[1]   Emcke, C. (2016) *Gegen den Hass*, Berlin: S. Fischer.

me the most was not the destination itself but the journey to hell!

'Well, I guess one needs to look at the issue as a puzzle', I began.

'A puzzle?'

'Yes. When I was a kid I suffered from a long illness. My mum bought me a puzzle of a German shepherd dog. It was a huge puzzle—2,000 pieces if I remember rightly. Most of them looked alike to me, either black or brown. But day after day, with patience, we managed to assemble the pieces.'

'Sorry, that's very interesting,' said the passenger, obviously struggling to remain polite, 'but how does it relate at all to anti-globalisation? I'm quite amazed with the serendipity of life, you see. I also spent my childhood building puzzles.'

Far from letting my fellow passenger lead me off track, I went on.

'You see, from afar, when you open the box,' I explained, 'the number of pieces and the task at hand seems daunting. Each piece seems identical to all the others and you can't see the contour of the dog or the grass and the image is blurred. But as you start working on it things come together. Success comes from recognising that each piece is unique and in understanding its contribution to the whole. Think about anti-globalisation and the rejection of trade and the migrants associated with it. The fear of migrants is partly the result of not being able to distinguish or see the human beings belonging to such an abstract construct. Language plays an important role here. Categorisation is a powerful tool, but it keeps all pieces together in a way that may blur our understanding.'

'Fine, but this is far too abstract for a politician or for society to use to address anti-globalisation issues, don't you agree?'

I nodded. 'Yes, that's why, like a puzzle, we can start working out the contour of the image, the 90 degree right angles first…'

'And these are?'

'Start with the fact that for most of our history on Earth we lived as a nomadic species', I said.

'Yes, but we no longer are', he interrupted. 'And people are afraid of losing their own culture and the traditions that have been transmitted from generation to generation. Don't you think that globalisation should be a process respectful of tradition?'

'Maybe, you're right', I mused. 'This is, after all, what we're afraid of losing—our memory of who we were when we were growing up. But tradition itself, you see, is the result of previous exchanges among our ancestors. It's even written in our DNA! But we've forgotten. Our capacity to transmit to our children what the result of *Otherness* was and make it ours, spanning longer or shorter periods, is the true wonder of the world!'

'Ah this is *still* too abstract for me!' said the passenger forcefully, but not without a hint of a smile.

'Maybe a first concrete proposal then would be to create a sort of traceability. Like we did when the mad cow epidemic occurred, do you remember? We traced the origin of the meat we ate. The goal was twofold. To regain trust and to provide more information to consumers. Cultural traceability would work the same way. By providing consumers with information about where products come from, not just geographically but also *historically*, we may make salient and palpable the otherwise abstract idea that our traditions are themselves the result of previous encounters between groups, societies and individuals, sometimes from far away.'

'Ah encounters!' exclaimed the passenger. 'Indeed, today we no longer refer to the discovery of America, but to the encounter between native populations, Europeans and African populations.'

'Exactly!'

'But once we know where goods come from, does it really provide a way to deal with global issues?'

'Well it provides an understanding of the interconnectedness between *us* and *them* and it builds the contour for building a global identity.'

'Ah! But why do we need a global identity? And, I can tell you straight away that I don't want to renounce my British identity!'

My fellow passenger looked at me with wide eyes, perhaps — inside — very annoyed by my proposal of building a global identity. *Touchy words,* I thought to myself. Happily, at that moment the ticket controller came to us asking for our tickets, thus saving me from my passenger's irritation. It gave us a moment to pause, and I took advantage of it to go to the bar-wagon. Trying not to sound upset, I asked him:

'Would you like a tea or a coffee?'

'No thanks, I'm fine', he said, curtly.

Minutes later, as I came back down the carriage from the bar-wagon with a tea in hand, I saw my fellow passenger once again reading the newspaper. He looked worried, and I wondered to myself if I wanted to keep talking with him, afraid that we might enter into conflict. Should I just sit far away and avoid the discussion? What should I do? Finally, I decided to retake my seat, all the time trying not to disturb him, sipping my hot tea and looking through the window at the passing landscape.

'What do you do for a living?' he asked, suddenly.

'I'm a professor of economics', I replied, looking at him.

'Ah! Economics! You know—I don't trust economists very much.'

'Why not?' I asked, intrigued by such provocation. Interested too in what he had to say.

'Well, all these studies saying that globalisation is good for growth: but still people are rejecting it! And think about it. How can economists really measure the causal impact of, for example, migration inflows? For instance, migrants may choose to move to countries where prosperity is high and therefore may be found not to have a negative impact, even if the counterfactual would have been that without migration prosperity would have been even higher or differently distributed!'

'You're right', I replied, surprised by his grasp of the subject. 'But economists often say correlation doesn't mean causation. And this is something that economists take very seriously. Let me give you one example of some research that manages to disentangle the two. It also provides evidence that migration inflows are not detrimental to the local economy.'

My fellow passenger stretched his legs, as if getting ready to listen to me—or rather *bear with me*, I thought.

'You see, one of the problems of looking at the correlation between labour market conditions and immigrant inflows is that, usually, migrants choose where to locate as a function of those labour market conditions.'

'So it's a chicken and egg problem!'

'Yes, you might say so. To address this problem, researchers try to find natural experiments.'

'Natural experiments?'

'That's right. These are historical events that lead to a random and unpredictable change in circumstances that allow researchers to answer a question. In the case of migrants and labour markets, a famous article[2] has exploited the decision of Fidel Castro to allow Cubans to freely emigrate to the US in April 1980. Half of the migrants settled in Miami, representing a massive—and politically determined—inflow of migrants into the city. The article analysing this event showed that there was no negative impact on the wages or labour market outcomes of the local population.'

'Really? How can that be possible?'

'A simple supply and demand argument! While immigrants increased the supply of labour, they also represented an increase in the demand of goods and services, and therefore the demand for labour, by companies located in Miami. You see, the pie is not fixed!'

'But weren't there bad consequences for the unskilled workers already living in Miami?'

'Economists have engaged in a controversy to answer this question.[3] Indeed, answering this question depends on thinking about the labour market outcomes of different groups, and taking into account pre-existing changes in the labour market, for instance in relation to female labour force participation. It also depends on the surveys used, since there may be reasons why certain populations are under-represented in surveys. Empirical work is challenging you see!'

'But from a theoretical point of view, why do you think that closing borders is not the answer?'

'Well, you see,' I answered, 'as I used to tell my students, some challenges span borders. They do not stop at the

---

[2] Card, D. (1990) The impact of the Mariel boatlift on the Miami labor market, *Industrial and Labor Relations Review*, 43 (2).

[3] Merler, S. (2017) The Mariel boatlift controversy, *Bruegel blog post*, 43 (2), (January 1990).

frontier. And it's not something we can remedy by building a taller wall. It's something that results from the fact that certain goods are simply non-rival.'

'Yes, but are these important goods?'

'Well, they're among the most important ones!' I said. 'Ideas are non-rival for instance, and we know they're a key source of prosperity. Peace is non-rival too, and I surely don't need to elaborate on why peace is essential for the economy to function properly. And many environmental goods are also non-rival. And not only are they non-rival but they're also non-excludable and global. And how much we collectively contribute to these public goods depends partly on how much we trust others, or on the extent of social capital!'

'Does opening our borders help us then?' said the passenger, almost warily.

'Well, from a dynamic point of view we know that closing borders decreases contact, which contributes to creating *Otherness* and makes society less likely to interact with others and to internalise the costs and the benefits of our actions onto others. This makes us less likely to change and less adaptable in the future. Indeed, trade in the past has shaped our "identity" today. By defining social capital at a local level, we make our communities less able to cooperate with other communities, we decrease our tools for solving problems globally. When we fail to identify with others, regardless of their origin, regardless of their identity, we lose track or we lose interest in their condition. Living in a world where national identity confers individuals with certain rights and makes them not accessible to others is living in a world of inward-looking gated communities.'

I stopped for a moment, realising that maybe I was getting carried away by the subject, and checked that my fellow passenger was still listening.

'Also,' I continued, tentatively, 'there's a key issue regarding the fact that, fundamentally, globalisation defines a global or at least supranational domain, and yet, the existing political and economic answers that we hear in many countries seem to be on a local or a national level. But the fact that the domain of globalisation is global doesn't mean that global or interconnected markets can function well without institutions, like states. Indeed, there's substantial consensus on the idea that markets and states are actually complementary. But, in this case, there's a mismatch between the domain of globalisation and the domain of state governance!'

'So should we just close borders, build new supranational institutions, or build a new global identity?'

'One proposal would be to allow for more human mobility. I think this should be a priority on world leaders' agendas—framing migration not as a threat but rather as a major opportunity to create prosperity for the largest number of people. Think of it—lack of labour mobility is one of the major economic frictions in the world today. Individuals who can move would naturally arbitrage between what countries have to offer in terms of political economic, cultural and environmental freedoms. Of course, societies that impose borders and that restrict migration outflows are trying to control their population and protect their national power structures. But those that restrict migratory inflows need to create their citizens' national identity to justify their action. Because mobility would undermine the power of rulers to oppress their citizens nothing is *really* done to promote it.'

'I know I mentioned how much I disliked the idea of creating global identity,' said the passenger, holding up a hand, 'but it's an interesting point. In your view, how could we go about creating it?'

'Well, first it's essential to recognise that our identities are multiple. Having a global identity doesn't eliminate your feeling of belonging to your neighbourhood, your city, town, region or your country.' The passenger looked at me. I couldn't exactly tell if he was really receptive to what I was saying, but I decided to continue. 'You see, schools shape our identity from childhood, allowing states to impose a psychological cost on individuals from leaving their countries. And that's exactly why societies or powerful groups are defiant of threats to what constitutes their vision of another's identity. As the famous historian Yuval Noah Harari[4] explains, this sense of national belonging helped former tribes to unite and overcome coordination problems that our ancestors faced, which in turn allowed them to build different types of infrastructure. Today, our world has become smaller, and nationalism is no longer the answer. In a world in which each individual has the right to decide what constitutes one's identity, we may freely experience how our identity may be nourished by where we live, what we do, where we work, who we pass in the street, but also by our migratory experiences. Regardless of whether we move or not, we need to explain that those characteristics do not constitute our humanness. Slaves were not less human than other humans even if they were treated like that. Minorities were not less worthy when they were condemned —or still are—as criminals in some countries.'

'So you're proposing to allow individuals to vote with their feet, basically, aren't you?' said the passenger, thoughtfully.

---

[4]   Harari, Y.N. (2014) *Sapiens: A Brief History of Humankind*, London: Vintage.

'Yes, exactly. Allowing individuals to vote with their feet and implementing an international order for open border policy might ease tensions today and tomorrow, and may be a way to democratise the world. This is the case both today —because it may ease the pressure on certain communities and therefore the risk of conflict—and tomorrow—because the more migration there is, the less likely it is that the *Other* is created, invisible and bundled into some sort of homogeneous group that supposedly poses a threat to our society.'

'But what's the responsibility of academics in all this? Is it only the politicians who are to be blamed?'

For some reason, perhaps the tone of his voice, I realised that my fellow passenger must work in politics. So I asked: 'Are you a politician, by any chance?'

He raised his eyebrows and sat back. 'Aren't we all to an extent? Well, yes,' he continued, 'for most of my professional life I've been heading up parents' associations and sitting on the local council of my district in Paris. You see, not so long ago, an old abandoned building in the heart of our community was supposed to have been transformed into a multimedia library for the inhabitants. Indeed, we fought hard to make this happen—the district desperately needed it. And then, in the summer of 2015, at the height of the migrant issue in Europe, a group of them—some hundred and fifty in the beginning and one thousand five hundred later—occupied the building with the help of an association. And we lived through the situation of tension ourselves—on the one hand, a large number of local inhabitants, including myself, were sons of migrants or first generation migrants. We felt we needed to organise and help them, and provide them with basic products, food, clothes, but also lobbying the politicians to provide the means to improve their living conditions by bringing sanitary facilities. And at the same time, while we got to know the migrants and work with them, we felt really infuriated by the inaction of the city and the fact that the library project was put on hold after all our efforts. We felt left behind, supporting too big a share of the burden of the migratory crisis, while we as a neighbourhood were already struggling compared to other well-off districts in the city. Some parents also became scared for their children's safety, as the school was just in front of the building occupied by the migrants, even if no violence occurred except among the migrants themselves. One of my neighbours, a sociologist, has recently published a book about this event, transmitting how complex our collective reaction was, triggering at the same time solidarity and fear, a sense of local injustice and an understanding of injustice on a broader global scale.'[5]

My fellow passenger came to a halt, paused, and looked at me with something approaching nostalgia in his eyes. I felt he might be wondering where some of those migrants he had helped were now.

'Do you think you could share the reference for the book with me—I'd like that', I said, feeling closer to him now. 'In fact, I'm even thinking of writing a book about globalisation and migration flows.'

He nodded. 'Why not—a pleasure. But I'm sure we'd all learn more by being in the field and experiencing such things. You know, I sometimes feel academics should be less into words and more into action—but don't let me discourage you to write that book', he added, leaning across to touch me lightly on the shoulder.

Suddenly, I realised how, through debate—even heated —we had come closer to each other on our journey to this

---

[5]   Coutant-Peyre, I. (2018) *Les migrants en bas de chez soi*, Paris: Seuil.

strange little town called hell. 'Well, academics certainly have the responsibility to think about the broader picture of things', I took up. 'Indeed, things can be improved on that front too. Much of the current analysis on globalisation aims at discussing the potential costs of globalisation for western societies, trying to explain the rise of extreme parties or populist parties. But as some economists have shown, many studies are only local by nature and static, failing to take into account the dynamic and global benefits—or costs—of opening—or closing—borders. But I believe that not only research but also primary and secondary education should be rethought. Our education systems throughout the world should focus much more attention on the exchanges that have taken place—migratory flows, forced and voluntary, knowledge flows, and our common attributes rather than teaching the history of particular countries.'

My fellow passenger nodded, remained thoughtful, and when he raised his head again his face lit up with a smile.

'Look! It seems that we're arriving at Enfer soon. You know, despite our differences, I'd like to keep in touch. You wouldn't want to share phone numbers, I suppose?'

At first silent, perhaps a little surprised, I also felt empathy for my new acquaintance and promised myself I would contact him when back from Enfer.

I always fall asleep when a journey is about to end, and this time was no exception. As my fellow passenger left to pick up his luggage further down the carriage, I laid my head on the window and went day-dreaming off to my old professor in Valparaiso. And in my dream I saw myself walking the steps down from the hill to her house… and entering through the open window, I found myself floating softly into her mind…

Chapter 10
Valparaiso, Chile

Ah, Valparaiso! After all these years of dreaming about coming here… Henri's house looks as majestic as I remembered it. Henri, my dear uncle, having emigrated to Chile all those years ago, and who'd been so kind as to leave me it. Today, I will have to clean the spider webs and get some boxes unpacked. The economics books that I didn't want to leave behind… all these years, teaching and transmitting knowledge.

Everything was very well organised. Each box had a name in it: *econ books, novels, travel books,* but also *clothes, silver-ware…* One box caught Martha's attention because no name was written on it. Had she forgotten? She decided to open that box first, maybe out of curiosity, maybe out of education —as a researcher, always trying to ask the questions that remain unsaid rather than answering already existing questions. As if the work of a researcher isn't really to answer them—a daunting task—but rather to shape the contours of knowledge through the process of asking new questions. The contours of a puzzle.

My graduation gown! I kept it for so many years in this box that I forgot about it. And I forgot to give it a name during the move.

Martha decided to take it out of the box and to clean it meticulously. Music by Christa Ludwiq was melting into the air as if accompanying each of her gestures.

I should clean it once a month and not keep it in a box anymore. She was repeating, without knowing it perhaps, uncle Henri's ritual: cleaning his gala uniform every month.

Opening an old antique closet, she checked whether the gown would fit well and remembered her graduation journey. At that time, she thought she had ended her learning journey but it was just starting. This she had come to understand when she retired. A teacher is a life-long student after all.

A soft and mysterious breeze entered the bedroom and caressed her skin. In a drawer hidden at the bottom of the closet she found a dusty old vinyl record of Chavela Vargas and a pack of handwritten notes. They were Henri's notes! Martha stopped cleaning the gown and left it on top of the bed, suspended in time and memory by Henri's words calling to her from the past.

'Pablo Neruda came up yesterday to let me know that Zoilo has passed away. His magnificent Stradivarius disappeared. How sad, Pablo told me, that he never played it, not a single time.'

Would my knowledge also disappear when I die? thought Martha. *Would it be left in a drawer unused, unread, waiting for it to be played?* She paused for a second, thinking about these questions while looking at the white curtains that were floating in the air as if someone was dancing with them.

Wandering in her thoughts and probably still jet lagged, the old professor fell asleep in a corner of the bed with the breeze entering the room and the gown lying next to her, and Henri's notes in her hands.

How odd this dream was. I could hear my former student and Henri talking together. But they belong to different generations! Did my student come to Valparaiso? Or was I just dreaming and confusing the past and the present? Neruda's voice completed the trio, and I could see the three of them leaving the house and walking the stairs up the hill, to attend the funeral of the poet Zoilo Escobar. I couldn't tell if my imagination was playing a trick on me or if I was entering one of Neruda's poems. It was the warmest hour of the day, when each object radiates the heat it has accumulated. As I woke up and walked around the house I noticed nobody had come in, and that all was quiet, my gown still lying on the bed. Preparing tea, I decided to play Chavela's vinyl record, *Angelitos Negros*. As the sun was setting I left the house and walked up the steps to the old city. Valparaiso awakening in me what lies beneath the surface and out of time… as if each step allowed me to enter the inhabitants' souls. They are all born with earthquakes in their memory. A consciousness of change and temporality that has given them the architecture of their city and of their souls, a port open to the world and receiving the world, an identity built out of change and exchange, out of creation and destruction. And as I went up the steps, I felt in my own skin Neruda's saying that walking around the stairs of Valparaiso is like touring the world. I reached a small plaza where I found several cats lazily sleeping and a little girl playing with a basketball. Suddenly her older brother came and took the ball from her, making her burst into tears. And as the girl ran to get the ball back from her brother, and as their father shouted from inside their house telling them not to fight—that their favourite show was starting on TV—I felt transported to the past. I remembered my students and that story I told them about the basketball and about my then young boys, Sasha and Max. Whether in London, Paris, Enfer or Valparaiso, I thought to myself, the nature of goods defines our relation to the world and to others more than the other way around. Two children, anywhere in the world, will sit quietly watching their favourite show, while they will fight to hold the ball. Not because they're nasty to each other, but because the TV show is non-rival while the ball itself is a rival good. The rules of the game—that is, the institutions we design to allocate resources—may be different here and there, but the nature of goods and the goods of nature aren't. And as I left the plaza, I saw a little plaque with a verse from a poem of Zoilo Escobar that caught my attention. It read: "*Soy operario de armonia cosmopolita*"—which loosely translated means *I'm the maker of cosmopolitan harmony*. And as I went back to Henri's old house, which was now mine, a flow of workers and students were walking back home, flooding the streets which turned into a lively mixture of colour and sounds. Cosmopolitan souls, maybe that was all we needed, maybe that was the answer to the puzzle.

A few months later, all the boxes had been opened and their contents either thrown away or stored. Everything was quiet in the house and a daily routine was installing itself. I got to know the neighbours and the shops around the house and where I would find my fruits and vegetables. Retirement was here, quiet and gentle, and I was just starting to think about writing my memoirs. One morning, after going to the market, I opened the mailbox and found a big envelope which I couldn't resist opening while walking back to the house.

Dear Martha,

I hope you are well and that you settled in wonderfully in Valparaiso. Do you remember when we met in the bookstore? I'd found a train ticket to a town named Enfer—so odd that in English it meant 'Hell'. Well, I took a day off work and journeyed into the adventure. As it turns out, the trip turned out to be more interesting than the destination. I met an odd and interesting man, a politician, who took me into a discussion about anti-globalisation. And he convinced me, without knowing it, about writing the book I mentioned to you, about the nature of goods and the goods of nature. Well, here it is! I printed it, since I remember you prefer working with pen and paper, and would be happy to receive your feedback. Please take your time, I'm sure you must be busy reading a million different things and writing your memoirs. Have you begun working on that? Hope all is well and I look forward to hearing back from you. From Hell to Paradise, if I may say!

Warmly,

Your student, always.

I sat and looked at the stack of pages printed back in London and sent out to me by my former student reaching out to her old professor. And I thought about my memoirs. Indeed, I should start soon. Spurred by her question, I sat at Henri's old desk and started to write in a small-sized black-cover notebook. It started like this:

'I had the chance to grow up in a peaceful country, and benefited from an education system and family life that enabled me to build my own path. My father, though, lived through the Spanish Civil War. He had to stop schooling at the age of twelve. At that age he had no choice but to start working as a necessity entrepreneur, driving poultry from his rural town to sell it in Barcelona. He started using a cart, then a truck. I remember he once told me that when he left his village very early in the morning it was foggy and cold. Upon arriving in Barcelona, he would find himself happy and singing. My father is still alive. He is ninety years old and he now lives in Barcelona. Today, he makes the same trip on weekends, but in the opposite direction, from Barcelona to his village, Guissona. And nowadays Guissona has received a big inflow of migrants who work in a large agro-factory. Through my own history, my memories and memoirs, which I am writing today

from my uncle Henri's former house in Valparaiso, Chile, I have come to the conclusion that who we are today and our habits are a reflection of the extent to which we exchanged with others in the past. The same goes for a country and its trade relations with others, which allows societies to build bridges from the past, even the very distant past, into the present and the future. And thanks to this ability to trade, to move, to come and go in search of prosperity and well-being, which is deeply rooted in our human history, my father, and many other men and women, have changed the world and have changed themselves.'

www.ingramcontent.com/pod-product-compliance
Lightning Source LLC
Chambersburg PA
CBHW061747270326
41928CB00011B/2409